Joy Comes in the Morning

Tara Talabi

PNEUMA SPRINGS PUBLISHING UK

First Published in 2022 by:
Pneuma Springs Publishing

Joy Comes in the Morning
Copyright © 2022 Tara Talabi
ISBN13: 9781782284918

Tara Talabi has asserted her right under the Copyright, Designs and
Patents Act, 1988, to be identified as Author of this Work

British Library Cataloguing in Publication Data. A catalogue record for
this book is available from the British Library.

Pneuma Springs Publishing
A Subsidiary of Pneuma Springs Ltd.
7 Groveherst Road, Dartford Kent, DA1 5JD.
E: admin@pneumasprings.co.uk
W: www.pneumasprings.co.uk

DEDICATION

To

Ayomide and Aramide,

My delightful chalk and cheese. Thank you for being born and giving me a reason to carry on!

ACKNOWLEDGEMENTS

I am fully persuaded that my decision to write this book was timely and directed by God. People were placed around me to spur me on and add flight to my wings as I soared while developing this script. With this in mind, I will like to acknowledge the following people:

Rebecca Timms, you read my first paragraph and assured me it was the start of a great book.

Karen McGovern, my very first amateur editor, you encouraged me, cheered me on and celebrated me every step of the way.

Kelly Thompson, you patiently listened as I went on and on about the manuscript and you checked up on its progress throughout the process.

My brother Timi Afanu, not only are you present in so many of the pages of this book, you proof read the first part of the manuscript and gave me the thumbs up. You also refused to rest until the photograph on the book cover was just right, thank you.

Joke Ayoade, my one and only Jokiyoyo, my sister and friend and Nigerian emissary, thank you for your encouragement and your support with the manuscript.

My cousin, Professor Funmi Lesi, whose intellectual input highlighted the nuggets within the manuscript, thank you Sis.

Dipo Akinrinlade, thank you for your enthusiastic encouragement, it fuelled my desire to complete the book.

Pastor Bose Odulele, thank you for carving out time from your busy schedule to read and write a review.

My baby girl Aramide, for putting up with my continuous requests to read out pages of the manuscript aloud to me.

My publishers, Pneuma Springs, I hope I didn't cause you too much trouble, thanks for your indulgence and bringing the book to its final conclusion.

Thank you Lord, I am eternally grateful!

CONTENTS

INTRODUCTION

As we emerge from the fog of Covid-19 and the numerous lockdowns, social distancing, face-masks, rule of six, plan B, hand sanitisers, PPE and all the new terms we have learnt along the way as we embraced this new way of living, it is with gratitude to God that I am still standing and still have my friends and family around me. So many people have gone! It was with this in mind that I gained a new appreciation for life and decided to take a more proactive stance in my day-to-day living.

For many years, my life has been all about my children. Bringing them up the best way I could, giving them all that I had to give. Their very existence spurred me on in life, they made life for me worth living. They are both young adults now and not so reliant on me as they once were, and I feel the time has come for me to explore other avenues in life to contribute to and in which I can give back.

I start by telling my story of how the dark clouds came unexpectedly and covered my sunshine. How in the midst of grief, sadness, pain, loss and weeping that may have endured for the night-time, the Lord restored joy in the morning. *Joy Comes in the Morning* is a brief account of my life's journey up to the age of fifty: the sharp bends in the road travelled, the valleys, the mountains, the oxbow lakes and the breasting of the tape to victory. The journey hasn't ended yet: a new chapter has just opened, and I am certain there will be more mountains to climb and victories to be won.

Chapter 1

Across the Atlantic

It was July 1978, and I was seven years old. My brother and I had boarded the plane at Stansted Airport, London, and it headed straight for Lagos, Nigeria. We had left our parents behind and travelled unaccompanied. We stepped off the aeroplane into what seemed to be a solid wall of humid heat. It was a contradiction of sorts, as the day seemed grey and overcast and looked as if it were about to pour with rain. We were met by relatives in Lagos and taken to my grandparents' home in Yaba. Their house was a lovely yellow bungalow in Moor Road, standing in the middle of a paved and gated garden. By the time we reached the house, the hot Lagos sun had come out in all its glory and dispersed all the murky grey clouds. As we opened the gate, three huge agama lizards scurried across the pathway and gave my brother and me a fright, since as far as we were concerned they were baby crocodiles! This was the beginning of my life in Nigeria.

After a few weeks my brother and I moved to Ibadan to live with my aunty and her family, where we were to begin school in September. My aunty, my dad's sister, was a matron in University College Hospital (UCH) and lived with her four boys and husband in Ibadan. She had prepared us for primary school: our uniforms, school-bags and school-shoes were ready for us.

Primary school in Ibadan was very different from school in the UK. My school was called Orita-Mefa Baptist Primary School. Staff all walked about with a cane in their hands or tucked in the middle of a book and their heads held high, as if they were some kind of demigod to be feared and revered. The children, however, were the same as children anywhere, ever ready to make fun of anything that was peculiar or different from what they were used to. Being the new girl in class was quite daunting, especially because most of the children spoke Yoruba as a first language and English as a second language. Luckily, I understood Yoruba because I had heard my parents speak it often, although I could not speak it. So when a child in my class shouted across the room in Yoruba,

'Hey, new girl, what's your name?' just to make sure I understood, I repeated the question in English, and that was the button pressed to take the mick!! Obviously, my English words came out with an English accent, and, as far as the children in my class were concerned, regardless of the colour of my skin, I was as English as Queen Elizabeth II. There were shouts of *oyinbo pepper*, which was colloquial for 'posh white'. I willed the floor to open up and swallow me whole. The children came closer and wanted me to speak again just so they could hear my accent. They goaded and taunted me to speak until a teacher came over to disperse the crowd. That afternoon, I went home and was determined to speak Yoruba from then on. Within a year in Nigeria, I was speaking Yoruba fluently.

I was quite new to a system wherein your class work was graded with numbers and you were given a numbered position in the class based on what your overall percentage grade was. Not only that, if you didn't get up to a certain grade you were asked to repeat the year! Can you believe it? This London child, at the end of the autumn term, was seventy-third out of seventy-five children! Diabolical indeed! My excuse was that I was missing my mother and didn't understand the language, and being in a strange country was just too much for me to handle at the time;

but I settled down and learnt to listen and realised that, since everything I wrote down was scrutinised, I woke up. At the end of the next term, my position was thirty-fifth out of seventy-five. I didn't stay in Ibadan long enough to get to number one in my year.

I lived in Ibadan with my aunty's family for about two years, until my parents returned to Nigeria from the UK and I moved back to Lagos, where we lived for many years. Once again, I started a new primary school, Ire-Akari Estate Primary School, and this time I was a seasoned Nigerian child and there was no teasing in sight. It was yet another eye-opener. The primary school was one of the new Jakande initiatives at the time. From the outside it looked like an arrangement of cow sheds, but, to be fair, the individual sheds had all the tables, chairs and blackboards that were needed to call them classrooms. It had the biggest windows you've ever seen, glassless and frameless, just a big space on top of the wall and beneath the roof, but we were never cold and never really wet: the design worked! Once again, our teachers walked the corridors with their heads in the air and a cane in their armpits to inflict their version of discipline on any children that did not obey the rules. It was also the place I discovered what was called a pit latrine. Goodness, the thought of it gives me shivers to this day! It was literally a small round hole in a concrete floor! I was informed that I was lucky that it was for single occupancy, as there were other places where there was a row of holes in the floor with no privacy. Needless to say, in my two years in that school, I never used the toilet while I was at school: whatever it was had to wait till I got home.

My stay in primary school was coming to an end, and to proceed to a decent secondary school you had to take what was called a 'common entrance' exam. If you passed, you would gain entry to any federal government college of your choice. In those days, they were good secondary schools. All primary six children in my school were registered for the exam and issued a slip with their exam number clearly displayed. You needed the slip to sit the exam. I, however, in the course of the day lost my slip. I got home and did not mention it to my mother. A couple of days before the exam my mother got to know from a friend that we should have received a registration slip with my exam number on it. My mother was livid to hear that I had lost it, but it was too late to get another one issued. For this reason I missed the exam that year and had to wait for an assessment the following year to gain entry into Federal Government Girls' College Bakori in 1982. So off I went in an aeroplane to secondary school in the northern part of Nigeria: yet another learning curve! Here there was no mummy, daddy, aunty, uncle, brother or cousin. But I quickly learnt to make sisters of the numerous students in my year-group and hostel. I was homesick, and having to shower in freezing cold water was a horrible ordeal but not optional. We all did it. We learnt to wash our knickers, brush our teeth and wash our entire body with one small bucket of water daily. Believe me, it was a life-skill!

Secondary education in a boarding-school certainly had its merits, even though it didn't seem so at the time. As boarders, we lived within strict boundaries which were supposed to be for our own good, to instil discipline and life-skills - which it probably did. As in any school, the entire day was mapped out by a timetable. Every minute of the day was accounted for. We woke up at around 5am, had a wash and did a morning chore. Everyone had an early morning job that had to be done before breakfast at 7am and to attend assembly immediately afterwards. School started at 8am and finished at 2pm. Then there was lunch, a compulsory siesta, afternoon activities, dinner-time, then evening prep (study-time) and finally bed-time; lights out at 10pm. As I write now, it conjures up warm memories that make me smile. Once, I had a maths teacher who came from Bangladesh, brilliant but not so patient with giggling thirteen-year-old girls. He would explain some long-winded mathematical equation on the blackboard with a piece of white chalk, which he would promptly drop, dust off his hands, turn around from the board and face us the pupils. He would then ask, 'Do you understand'? There would then be a chorus of yeses and noes. He would then calmly respond to us, that the no-girls should meet the yes-girls, and that was it! Many a lesson was taught to me by the yes-girls.

Tara Talabi

Chapter 2

Back to the Beginning

My parents came to the UK in the early 60s and were students on Commonwealth Scholarships when I was born. My father was studying marketing at Lambeth College, and my mother was doing her internship in a pathology lab in Queen Mary's Hospital, Roehampton. So it seemed only right that when I came along I should be born there. I came along towards the end of the summer of 1970, and I was a total delight and joy to my parents! My father for one desperately wanted a baby girl, as he believed it was good fortune to have a daughter for a first child, and his prayers were answered.

In just under two years following my arrival, my brother was born, and for the next few years we were like two peas in a pod. We were Tara and Timi and hardly appeared anywhere one without the other. We went to childminders together, nursery together and even Fair Croft Infants and Juniors, Tooting Bec, together. I was the big sister, slightly bossy, I must confess, and he was my baby brother, and at that age I genuinely thought that it would always just be the two of us. I was told by my mother that I was quite jealous of him when he first arrived in our home in 1972, because he was put in my old cot and was fed with a baby's feeding bottle. Even though I no longer used these things, I remembered them and promptly claimed them back: they were mine first, after all; but once I was assured that they belonged to me but should let the baby use them, that was totally acceptable.

We grew up together sharing everything. Timi was certainly my first best friend, and that bond exists to this day. In 1977, we both went on holiday to the Netherlands and stayed with our aunty and her husband for the duration while we enjoyed the city of bicycles. When we returned to the UK, as if by magic, our mother was heavily pregnant. Somehow we hadn't noticed this five weeks before, when we left. I wasn't sure whether to be excited by this impending baby or not. The prospect of someone else joining our family was slightly unsettling, and I thought it would be great only if the baby were a girl. In my mind, that would be a good balance: I should have a brother and a sister.

One afternoon, my brother and I had just returned from school. I had the house-key on a chain round my neck and, at the tender age of seven, was in charge of bringing my five-year-old brother back home from school and making us both some toast before my mother got back from work. Things were certainly different in those days. The telephone down in the hallway rang. I picked it up and recited our telephone-number to the caller, with a 'How can I help you?' at the end: this was how we did it in those days. It was my father calling to announce that we had a new baby brother, and I forgot all about balance and was just excited that we had a baby. I quickly decided to be its little mummy, and all was good with the world until it was time for Timi and me to relocate to Nigeria. My parents had decided it was time for them to go back home to Nigeria. They had been in the UK for close on twenty years. Their parents missed them and most of their contemporaries that came over to study in the UK in those days had returned to Nigeria. It was never the plan to stay away for so long. The plan was to get an education, return home, and start putting down roots in the homeland. The education part was sorted, it was time to go home. Their plan was to send us ahead and to get us settled in school before they joined us at the end of the year.

I remember being very excited to get a passport-photograph taken and to make the journey to the Nigerian embassy to apply for the green hardback passport. I even remember getting our travel vaccinations done. They weren't fun but definitely a requirement for travelling. Shopping with my mother was also exciting, getting all the correct gear together for this adventure. At the time, it didn't occur to me that we would actually be separated from our parents and our home. The time came soon enough, and we boarded a plane at Stansted airport.

Chapter 3

Life as an Undergraduate

We lived in Lagos, a bustling city no matter which part of it you lived in. I was proud to be a Lagosian. No other city I visited in Nigeria could hold a candle to Lagos. It had a certain kind of vibe that existed only in Lagos. It had its own sounds and smells that welcomed me from the airport when I arrived back from secondary school at the end of each term: the sounds of the sliding doors of the local combi-bus and the bus-conductors shouting their different destinations and the constant squabble of how the change in coins was to be shared out. It also had a unique stench, a combination of stagnant gutters, car-pollution and street-food. If you smelt it long enough, it became quite pleasant.

It seemed I always had to leave home to gain an education. For secondary school, I left home and went up north, but for university I was back down in the south, not in Lagos but in Ile-Ife, Osun State. My mother's sister was a mathematics professor and lectured at Obafemi Awolowo University, my *alma mater*. When she unfortunately died while I was in my first year, I had to find myself a new university mother to look out for me while I was there. I gained admission in December 1988 to study Management Accounting, which was my dream course and first choice, but life at university just made me yearn to return to the UK. By this time, I was an adult and saw and perceived things in a more mature fashion than when I was younger. I could see injustice and corruption, and a lot of it just made me cringe.

One great thing that I experienced at uni was meeting Christ and becoming a Christian. My transition was slow and hesitant, but once I gave in, I never looked back. Before I finally gave in, I had seen many versions of Christianity, and not all of them were encouraging. Some looked as if they physically carried the sins of the world on their shoulders: haggard and miserable, and there was no way I was signing up for that. Another group looked as if they were the most holy group in the world and could not cough without taking permission from God. This also to me was not attractive. I felt as if joining them would be going from one type of bondage to another.

I still had a huge desire to follow Christ, and so I did it my own way. I sought out my salvation by myself. In the privacy of my room I had accepted Christ into my heart but still wanted to be called to the altar and make a public surrender. I attended one of the campus' main churches. There were two, a Roman Catholic one and a Protestant one. The Protestant one was called All Souls Chapel and catered for a combination of Protestant denominations. At the time there were about six different vicars that conducted Sunday worship, one after the other. Of the six, there were two that, whenever they led worship, always made an altar-call at the end and I noted who they were for future reference. On the day I finally decided I needed to make my public declaration, I had prayed the night before that God should please make one of those two vicars take the service at All Souls Chapel the next day, so that, when they made the call, I should be ready to respond.

On that bright Sunday morning, I woke up extra early to give myself enough time to get ready and paid particular attention to how I dressed and how I looked generally, knowing that today was the day I was going to the altar. I got to church early enough to choose a convenient place to sit, somewhere where I could get up easily and not have to press past many seated congregants in the pews. I was slightly nervous, because at this point the vicar hadn't come out of the vestry, so I wasn't quite sure which vicar was on duty for the day. I gave a sigh of relief and a 'thank you, Jesus' when the right vicar came out and we stood up to start worship. That morning, in All Souls Chapel Ile-Ife, an altar-call was made, and I was the only one that came out. My heart rejoiced because I knew the angels in heaven were cheering me on and that this was the beginning of another journey in my life.

I was in year one - 'one hundred level', as we used to call it. I had done a philosophy test, and our lecturer was handing out our marked test-sheets. He called your uni registration number, and you went up to collect your sheet. When he called mine, I went to collect it, expecting some pretty decent grade something like in the 70 percentile is what I was expecting. When I collected the sheet, I had got 46%! I was heart-broken, and it must have shown on my face. My lecturer looked at me and said, 'What, you don't like it? Come and see me in my office tomorrow morning so we can discuss it,' to which I replied, 'okay, sir. Thank you, I shall see you tomorrow morning.' How naïve could a nineteen-year-old be? At 8.30am prompt, I reported to his office and had the shock of my life when he made a pass at me! To be fair, he didn't touch me in any way, but he implied that he could sort my grade out for certain favours. That's when it occurred to me what was happening and I realised what I had gotten myself into. I had the presence of mind to mention to him that I couldn't stay for long because I had to meet my aunty. As soon as he heard the name of my aunty, a very formidable character in the faculty of nursing, all bets were off. He immediately asked me to hurry along, and I never encountered him again. I learnt my lesson that day, to be careful who you smile with on campus and to scrutinise every offer.

I finally found a group of Christians that I could identify with. The ladies were not wearing head-scarves, long sleeves and long faces; neither did they seem to shun anyone who wasn't part of their Christian group but welcomed everyone with open arms and a smile. To me they seemed to be a happy bunch of ordinary people who loved the Lord and were not ashamed to share their love. They were called the Christ Lovers of The Christ Love Fellowship. I enjoyed growing as a Christian with this group of people. I was fed and grounded in the Word over the years with this lot. I owe my foundation as a Christian to this group. God used them to form me into the Christian I am today, and I thank God for them.

I'll tell you a bit about them. If you were a real member, you would have to take a membership-class over five weeks or so. It didn't matter what level of Christian you were. Christ Love Fellowship needed to tell you who they were, what they believed and how you were expected to live as a child of God. All the foundations of beliefs and doctrine were taught and put in place through these classes. At the end of the classes, you were mandated to join a department and be part of a smaller group to aid your growth and commitment. I joined Hospital Outreach. I was a shy girl and quite reserved and didn't want to join any group that was too much in the lime-light like Praise Creation, which was the choir group, or His Passion, which was the drama group. Whether Hospital Outreach was a good fit for me, I'm not quite sure, but I was part of them for a couple of years at least. We went to the local teaching hospital every Sunday morning to visit the patients, talk to them, pray with them, share the gospel with them and sometimes just listen to them. The group was divided out into the different wards, and we went armed only with our Bibles and a prayer. Some of the patients were happy just to have a visitor, some didn't want to see us at all, as they had given up on God. Some were eager for the gospel and gave their lives to Christ. Some were too sick to notice we were even there, and some just tolerated us because they had nothing better to do. We would spend about an hour and a half in the hospital and then return to campus. Most Sundays I returned to campus with a heavy heart and a drawn countenance and people kept on asking me whether I was okay. This was because I had seen sickness and suffering and hadn't learnt how to shield my soul, and so the fear and sadness of what I had seen on the medical wards had seeped in. When I realised what I was going through, I made a request to limit my visits to certain wards, like orthopaedic and neonatal. The patients there were not really on death roll, and the adults were more ready to listen to me and receive Christ when we visited.

Christ Love Fellowship was a big part of my life on campus. I didn't like the academic part of my stay in university because I was no scholar really and I had to work so hard for very meagre returns. But the independence of being away from home was glorious, and my spirit-man developed and soared. I got baptised in the Holy Spirit and learnt how to pray in tongues. This empowered me to make deep and powerful intercessions for my family and even for my friends. I loved attending prayer-meetings, and at one of them I noticed a handsome young man. Every time I went to fellowship, I saw him and noticed him. For me, this was quite unusual, because I wasn't in the habit of noticing young men. But this one I noticed. As I observed him, I realised he was very popular and quite friendly. Everyone knew him, and he seemed to be everyone's friend. He was an excellent prayer warrior and the pastor of the fellowship often deferred to him asking him if he had a special word from God for the congregation. Sometimes he did and sometimes he didn't. Nonetheless, this was a most attractive attribute to me.

This was a young man who truly knew and loved the Lord. Also, he could speak the Queen's English, and he presented very well. He was smart, tall and handsome; we'll call him Mr Handsome for now. I'm sure I wasn't the only one that noticed him. Further more, when I checked him out more closely, he ticked all the boxes that I hadn't even realised I had before then. Besides, one evening during fellowship when I was having a quiet moment with God about having a young man of my own, God actually whispered to me about considering Mr Handsome. It was so out of the blue, and even though I had noticed him, he wasn't my friend and he moved with the popular crowd of which I was not part. But I took God's word, and I considered him. I had a very short list of what I really wanted. Nothing too elaborate. He had to be a fabulous

Christian, and that was already a given. He had to be Yoruba and hail from the Ijebu tribe. My mother was from Ijebu and they were the Yorubas I really knew. (Since my father was a Lagosian, I couldn't really call him Yoruba.) Anyway, as it turned out, Mr Handsome hailed from Ijebu Imodi-Mosan, so that ticked another box. Finally, he had to have British citizenship because there were so many con-men out there just looking for a girl with British citizenship to marry and become British themselves. Yes, my Mr Handsome was born in Paddington in 1967; he was indeed British. But how on earth were we going to connect and come together? I was too shy to make the first move. So I decided just to trust God. If God had shown him to me, then he'd have to show me to him as well. I waited on the Lord; the seed was planted.

One day, over a holiday, I came to campus to attend a friend's convocation, and I bumped into Mr Handsome. We exchanged addresses and the seed germinated.

Life on campus continued for me, quite uneventfully. I took way too long to pass all my courses, and I thought graduating was the hardest thing I had ever achieved in my life! All through my stay, I made very few close friends. I had some friends that went to the same secondary school as I did, that stayed close, but in general I think I was rather aloof and didn't need many people to be happy. My university mother, as I referred to her, was Ms Kujore. She was my late aunty's best friend, and she took me under her wing when my aunty died. Her children, Ayo and Jumoke, and her niece Joke became my campus siblings and were my support network for most of my years on campus. Indeed they became my family for life and supported me through the good times and bad even after university.

My university - Obafemi Awolowo University, was its new name - had a very vibrant students' union and active students' council, and they were, at the drop of a hat, ready to protest over anything they deemed unfair happening on campus. There were riots and civil unrest over the simplest things, and often some serious issues as well. The sad thing was that we were all affected by the riots, whether we wanted to be part of them or not; whether we agreed with the protest or not. Occasionally there would be a protest rally held in the university's amphitheatre beforehand, to inform the student population of what the grievance was, but at other times there would be just a rumble: everyone was chased out of the lecture-theatres and instructed not to return until further notice. The phrase, *A luta continua; vitória é certa,* meaning, 'The struggle continues; victory is certain', was a popular term on the lips of students, and it just indicated that we were having another break from learning to stay at home until the matter was resolved.

During one such *A luta* break, at home and feeling bored, I decided to go and visit an old friend who lived on Victoria Island. It took me about two hours to get myself together: a shower, the right clothes, the right level of make-up to look the part of a successful undergrad on an *A luta* break. (In those days, we took pride in how we looked, and, if you were going into town, you wanted to look the part.) As soon as I stepped out of my front door, I didn't feel like going out anymore, but I had put too much effort into getting ready to give up now. So I carried on. I got on to one of our local buses that took me to a bus-depot where I would take another into town, but the feeling of 'go back home' persisted, so I gave in and returned home. When I got home, I changed into my comfy home-clothes, stretched myself out on the living-room sofa and began to read a novel that I had started to read the night before. I was there for only about ten minutes when there was a knock on the front door. To my most pleasant surprise when I opened the door, Mr

Handsome stood grinning at me in my doorway. He said he was passing by and decided to drop by and say hello! We spent the better part of the day together. We talked and shared stuff about each other; we shared scripture; we had lunch that I cooked; we laughed a lot. Some moments were serious, others light hearted, and at the end of the day my heart was truly smitten. I was totally hooked; but I kept this a secret. This information was for my heart only.

Chapter 4

Courtship

Mr Handsome had become my friend. His name was Temitope Abraham Talabi. Over the next few months we became great pals. We had lunch together once a week and spent the afternoon just talking and getting to know one another. At some point we returned to school when the *A luta* break was over and spent just a few weeks there, and then the semester was over. At last I had completed all the course requirements for me to graduate, and I was ready to leave Nigeria and return to the UK.

The day before I left Nigeria, Tope visited me at home, and we had lunch together, as was our custom. It was a weird farewell as I was returning to London the next day, and, even though Tope was planning to come to London as well, we had no idea when he would make the journey. At the end of his visit, just before he stepped out of my front door, he turned around to me and asked me if he could kiss me. This came as no surprise, as there had been a fair bit of tension in the air all afternoon. I was thrilled that he had chosen to ask me rather than just steal a kiss and make things awkward. Much as I suspected, his request had been for something more intimate, I turned my face to him and tapped my cheek. He hesitated for a second, then took my face in his two hands and gently placed a kiss on the peak of my left cheek bone, just under my eye. It was the most sensual feeling I had ever experienced in the whole of my twenty-four years! I knew I was going to marry him! First of all, God had whispered to my spirit about him, then we miraculously became friends, and now I'm dreaming about him at night! I had no doubt that God was willing and able to make it happen for us.

It was a crisp morning in the spring of 1995 when I returned to the UK. It had been about sixteen years since I left, and returning now felt like a long-awaited home-coming. Timi met me at the airport and brought me home to his flat in Sydenham. Everything felt familiar yet new at the same time. The red double-decker bus was familiar, but it was strange that I had to get on in the front by the driver instead of hopping on and off at the back like on the old route-master buses. Also there was no conductor: this too was new. The very next day I visited the social security office, where I had a brief interview and was issued with a national insurance number. This meant I could look for work and, while I was looking, get a weekly stipend from the giro office. I also went to our local GP's and registered. Within the first week of my return, I had become a legitimate Londoner, armed with my NI card, weekly travel card, weekly giro in my purse and even a new NHS medical card. I promptly started looking for work. Even though I had a first degree in accounting, I had absolutely zero work experience! While I was looking for work, I was offered a RSA course in word-processing with the further offer of finding me a job at the end of it. That was the attraction. At the end of the four-week course, I got a job on the post office counter with three weeks' training at the post office headquarters in Kent; and then I started the job at my local post office situated in the Sava Centre, Sydenham. That was my first-ever job, and I really loved it.

At this point, deciding to find myself a church, I got a list of churches I wanted to visit, possibly choosing one eventually to be my home church. At the first church I attended, where I met someone I knew, I was compelled to stay longer than I had planned. There was no hurry, however, so I stayed there for a couple of months; but I always knew that it wouldn't be home and that I would always be a visitor there. For the moment, though, it was fine. It was nice to mix with other young Christians who lived in London and were all beginning life: some students, some new workers and some had been here a good while and had settled into careers. We were all at different stages of our lives and this helped us encourage and spur one another along.

Then something great happened: Tope arrived from Nigeria! As mobile phones were not really popular at that time, staying in touch with him before he arrived from Nigeria was almost impossible, so his arrival in London was really a pleasant surprise. He lived with his brother in north London while I was with my brother in south-east London, but we didn't let the distance cause a problem. It was a two-hour journey from door to door, but we got to see each other almost every weekend. We picked up our friendship where we left off and, being in a strange country, we got even closer. We talked a lot. Tope was so easy to talk to. I found myself telling him everything about myself. Some things he would approve of and some he would tell me wouldn't do, and he would explain to me what the Bible said about certain things.

One day, Tope asked me if I had a boyfriend, and without hesitation I said, 'Yes'. I told him I had met the person I was going to marry and this seemed to bother him, just a little. He asked me who the person was, and I told him I wasn't ready to share that information yet. Then he asked whether it was someone he knew, and I confirmed that I did believe he knew him. For two weeks we went backwards and forwards over the identity of my mysterious boyfriend, when in all truth the person I was referring to was Tope himself! But I had to be sure that Tope's intentions were what I thought they were before I revealed my hand. After a lot of questions and answers, Tope was beginning to catch on that he was the man of my dreams. It wasn't rocket science really, because we spent all our spare time together: who else would it be? But I suppose he wanted to be certain as well, and so eventually I asked him just to tell me who he thought my heart-throb was, and he declared that it had to be he himself.

We wasted no time at all in declaring our love for each other and that we were to be married as soon as it could be conveniently arranged. There and then we decided we should be married in two years' time, in the hope that we should both be more settled and in decent jobs by that time.

One thing I quickly realised was, you lose a large portion of your independence when you get into a relationship. I had avoided any kind of steady relationship all my adult life for this very reason, but the good thing is, when you're in love, you're willing to do a lot of giving. So when Tope insisted I came to his church the following Sunday and meet his sister, even though it derailed my own plans for which church I wanted to attend that Sunday, I gladly gave in. On Sunday morning, off I went to Glory Bible Church in Leyton. Because there were train cancellations at London Bridge, I got to church a bit late - not a great start! However, I enjoyed every bit of the service and immediately knew that Glory Bible Church was to be my home church. Something peculiar happened while I was there. After the pastor finished preaching, there were some announcements by someone else, and then the pastor came back to take the offering. To my surprise, he had totally changed his attire. Even his shoes were different. It wasn't in itself an important point, but I did think it rather peculiar; maybe that was how it was done in London. After the service, there were a lot of people saying 'hello' to each other, groups of people laughing and chatting, and the general vibe felt very familiar. While all this was going on, I had to look twice when I saw two almost identical pastors. The pastor didn't change his attire to come and take the offering after all: they were actually twin brothers! That really tickled me. If I had done my homework before I attended the church, I should have known there were two of them. During all the lively meet and greet, I met Titi, Tope's sister, and she invited us to have lunch at her house that afternoon.

This was essentially the beginning of our courtship. It was hard work. I loved Tope dearly, but in character we were very different. We both loved the Lord passionately, and this helped to glue us together. We both believed that our union was of God and that we had not just randomly chosen each other; but we still battled with personal hopes and desires. For instance, I believed that a man should be 'butch', menacing, fierce, not to me but to anyone that threatened my space, whereas Tope was a gentle giant, and his aggression was buried so deep that it took a lot to make it show up. The men in my life, my dad and my brothers, were formidable characters and could hold their own in any kind of fight. Tope, on the other hand, wanted a wife who was slim and fair-skinned! Now, that just was not going to happen! I was never going to be slim or fair-skinned. I was and still am dark, fat and beautiful. He came round eventually. But it took work and determination. Also, the fact that I was so sure I heard from God regarding our relationship was a good foundation for me to stand on any time things seemed rocky. We had to work on each other's thought-patterns and attitudes. Tope always started with, 'This is what the Bible says', and then he'd dare me to disagree. Even though I would argue with him and make a fuss, most times I would come round to his way of thinking in the end. He taught me so many things, and I know he learnt a thing or two from me as well. We had a thorough courtship. I think we learnt everything that was possible to learn of each other without living under the same roof. We were old-time Christians: we had agreed to wait and do things in what we deemed was the right order. So while we waited, we did everything else. We prayed together daily, every morning over the phone, we went out to the cinema, to restaurants, to shows, just for a walk, to church, to weddings and parties and concerts; we had a great time. When we started planning our wedding, we agreed to have the whole ceremony here in the UK. None of our parents were living in the UK and would have to fly in for the event, but that would still have been cheaper than for us to have the wedding in Nigeria.

Chapter 5

Getting Married

Planning the wedding was very exciting. We didn't have lots of money, but we had a lot of friends as we belonged to a large and vibrant Pentecostal church. Tope generally agreed to whatever I wanted and let me choose our colour schemes, cake, rings, order of service, invitations and even reception agenda and he gave me as much money as he could to do whatever needed to be done. We had planned the wedding for a season when lots of weddings were taking place in Glory Bible Church, so we were all comparing notes and giving each other tips on which was the best way to go.

A week before the wedding, on a very sunny Saturday afternoon, I called a cab and loaded all my worldly belongings from my brother's house and took a drive up north to Tope's flat, which was soon to become my home too. On getting there, Tope was out, but he had left me a message on a post-it on the door. It said, 'There's cold water in the fridge'. This made me smile, because he knew how I loved cold water, and, on a hot day such as this one, it was exactly what I needed. I went straight to the fridge and yanked the door opened. To my surprise there, on the middle shelf, was a single long-stemmed red rose and a note saying, 'Welcome home'. I thought that was the sweetest thing ever!

Tope had an uncle who owned a restaurant, and he offered to cater for all the food at the wedding. He was aghast, however, to hear we were catering for 400 guests. In those days, you invited the whole church, so that's what we had done. He supplied what he could, and we sorted out the rest with the help of other friends and family that chipped in here and there.

On 27 September 1997, we were married at Glory Bible Church. I can sincerely say it was one of the happiest days of my life! Everything went according to plan on the day, at least with the ceremony. It was truly glorious. At last I was married to the love of my life. We had booked a hotel in which to spend our wedding night, down in south London so that we didn't have to go all the way back home till the next day. After we had wrapped up everything at the reception hall, we retired to the hotel. It was my wedding night after all. I was giddy with excitement with what was supposed to happen that night. This was something that with great restraint we had both wanted but chosen to wait to do. I had bought a pretty nightie and fabulously smelling shower-gel, and, even though I had been advised to buy some kind of lubricant, I decided to give that a miss, because I was so sure that I wouldn't need it. After a quick shower to wash off all the grime of the day, I put on my slinky little nightie, but it made very little impression on my husband as he was far more interested in what was beneath the pretty cloth. But I was a bag of nerves! Alas, now that I was fully licenced to take the drive, I was just too tense and wound up to let it happen. Even though I was the one that couldn't relax, I think I was more disappointed than Tope was. He assured me that all was well and that there was no hurry, we were married now and we had all the time ahead of us. I fell asleep in his arms, determined to try harder the next time.

The next day we boarded the Eurostar at Waterloo to Paris for our honeymoon. We were the typical tourists. Tope was excellent at things like these. Armed with a map of Paris, we ticked off the beautiful Parisian landmarks one by one over the next six days. We made sure we got to the top of the Eiffel Tower, had a boat cruise on the Seine, visited the Louvre museum - just to mention a few places - and we even spent one whole day at Euro Disney! During the day we were traipsing around the city; in the evenings we had dinner at one local fast-food joint or another, and at night we were in each other's arms, discovering the physical delights of being married.

After six days in Paris, we returned to the UK, where real married life began. Living with and loving Tope was so much fun. It was a learning curve, as we generally did things differently. But Tope was so calm and considerate. He wasn't like my dad, who was the king of the castle and made sure everyone knew it. Tope helped me to spread my wings, he encouraged me to talk more, to speak my mind, to discuss difficult topics, to be more assertive, to pray more, to study more, to take charge. He encouraged me to go places and make friends. In short, Tope's wife had to be a strong whole woman, one who could confidently stand independently on her own two feet, physically, spiritually and emotionally, and he groomed me to be that person. Tope told me every single day that he loved me, but for me the words never came that easily. I was more of an-action-speaks-louder-than-words kind of girl. Whenever I told Tope that I loved him, he would laugh and ask me why I said it. Tope also never believed that there were tasks for a woman or for a man. He believed if we were both able to do a task, then either one should do it. For instance, he didn't believe it was my sole responsibility to cook or wash the dishes: he was quite happy to cook any time I allowed it. And he quite happily on many occasions told me to go to bed and leave the dishes when he saw me yawning after dinner and he would wash them up. He in turn also expected me to climb up a ladder and change a light bulb if need be and would never have thought that I should wait for him to come and do it.

After being married for a few months, I started pining for a child, but we had agreed not to try for a baby until after a year of being married. We both believed we needed time to get to know one another properly and to put money aside for whoever was to join us. So when he refused to break our initial plan, I asked for a cat. Unsurprisingly, that received an even bigger No! We then decided to focus on our jobs and careers. Tope was doing exams to qualify as a Microsoft systems engineer, and I found my first job in an accounts office. Life was sweet. We still were not rich, but we were blissfully happy. We had good friends, a good church, decent enough jobs and a fabulous home life. We were both very committed to our church and attended multiple times a week as well as serving in different departments within the church. I was a member of the children's church, while Tope worked mainly with the new converts. We both came from Christ Love Fellowship in Ife and were raised not to be bench-warmers in church! A large percentage of the congregation were young people just like us, born in the UK, schooled in Nigeria, who had returned to the UK and loved and served the Lord, all of us making our way in life with dreams of grandeur in our future. It was good to be in the midst of like-minded people: it helped us to focus and strive to grow up and not be left behind.

A couple of months before our first year wedding anniversary, feeling quite ill, I suspected I might just be pregnant. I was excitedly mulling this possibility around in my mind and wondering whether we were economically viable for bringing a baby into this world. *God, please tell me, can we really afford a baby?* was the question in my heart. And God answered me in just a few minutes. I was getting ready for work early in the morning, and Premier radio was on in the background. The words came to me as if in direct answer to the prayer in my heart: *'I have been young, and I am now old; and I have not seen the righteous forsaken or his seed begging bread'*. Someone said it on the radio. It's a quote from

Psalm 37:25. I heard it and received it immediately, making room for it to dwell in my spirit. That was all I needed to be sure that we would be okay. I promptly shared this word with Tope but didn't tell him my news just yet. I needed to be sure. But it's the kind of news that is very difficult to keep to oneself. So my silence didn't even last the day. I called him at work and told him what I suspected, but he refused to get excited about it until it was confirmed, we agreed to get a test done as soon as possible. I went off to the GP to get a test done, and pregnancy was confirmed. My dear friend Funmi lived right next to the GP's, and I popped in to share my news with her.

Tara Talabi

Chapter 6

A Bun in the Oven 1.0

Expecting a baby should be a really exciting time in one's life. It's a time when one dreams of the baby and plans for it, prays for it, shops for it and generally makes changes and allowances for what is to come. I did all this. Even though the baby wasn't born yet, there were now three of us in the family. As I prayed daily for myself and my husband, I prayed for my baby too. It took only about two weeks of knowing I was expecting for the sickness to start. It's called 'morning sickness' in pregnancy, but I was sick all day! I was vomiting on average four times a day, which made me dehydrated and then gave me pain in my bones and ketones in my urine. I ended up with a condition called hyperemesis. It was awful. I had never been so sick in my life. I remember one morning on the way to work, I was vomiting in a side street, I must have looked as if I was hung over and on my way back from a rave. A woman came up to me, asked me whether I was pregnant and offered me some baby wipes to clean myself up. On another occasion, I was coming back from work and on the top deck of a bus, feeling totally dejected. I thought to myself, this should be a happy time, but it wasn't, I was not accustomed to being unwell, it was a totally alien feeling for me. My mouth tasted horrible, my body ached, I experienced dizziness off and on, and almost every smell nauseated me. This was really hard work! I sat on the bus and wept. I got home and crawled into bed for a proper cry when the house-phone rang. Now, trust me when I tell you that God works in mysterious ways, He is faithful and looks after his own. I had every intention of ignoring the phone, but something in me compelled me to pick it up. It was a cousin of mine, Cynthia. She said she just called to find out how I was. She had never called me before, and I don't think she has called me since, but on this fateful day she called. I cried, I told her I was fed up with being pregnant and sick and that I wanted to go home to my mother. She laughed. She told me I was already at home in my husband's house. She congratulated me that I was even able to be pregnant and go to work. She said when she was pregnant, from two months till the child was born, she was on bed-rest. She asked me if I had tried eating water melon; she said it might help. I was grateful for her call. I was encouraged that my case was not unique. I phoned Tope and asked him to buy a couple of water melons on his way home from work. For the next three months, I ate water melon for breakfast, lunch and dinner. It was the only thing I ingested that didn't come back up. Everything else, even water, found its way back.

I was due a normal antenatal visit to the hospital, which I took time off work to attend. I attended my appointment at Chase Farm Hospital. By the time they had finished doing my observations, weighing/ measuring, blood-pressure and urine tests, I was told they couldn't let me go back to work or even back home. I had to be admitted to the maternity ward and put on a drip straight away. Tope was called and asked to pack me a bag, which he did, but didn't remember to pack any knickers! I was in hospital for the next five days trying to get my fluids up. This happened on four other occasions while I was pregnant. I was constantly dehydrated because I was always vomiting. Apart from this condition, everything else was fine. No high blood-pressure, no gestational diabetes, no chromosomal abnormalities: for this I was thankful for the Lord's mercies. On my first wedding anniversary, when I was stuck in hospital attached to a drip, all my friends in church thought Tope had taken me on a romantic weekend away to celebrate!

After about five months of pregnancy, my condition started to improve. I had mastered what time I could eat and what I could eat that would save me from vomiting. At this time, it was only happening about once or twice a day. Black coffee or orange Lucozade were my drinks of choice. I had lost about 12kg in weight, but I was now beginning to feel normal. I started doing my baby shopping: this was one of the highlights of my pregnancy. Buying baby furniture, baby clothes and nappies was most exciting! I was working for a local magazine-distributing company, not too far from where I lived. It was one bus ride from home but on so many occasions I had to rush off the bus mid-way to work just because I had to vomit or because it was too stuffy and felt as if I was about to faint. I worked up till I was thirty-six weeks pregnant and then gave up and went on maternity leave. I thought that, because I was so heavily pregnant, I would give birth early and that baby would be very big; but as God would have it, at forty weeks I was still pregnant, and baby didn't seem to be anywhere near willing to come. At forty weeks and five days, my first-born child was born! Ayomide Morohunfoluwa Timothy Talabi was born at 6pm on 24 March 1999, weighing 7.1lb. He was truly gorgeous, and Tope and I were ever so grateful.

Ayomide was so easy to look after he made motherhood seem easy. In the early days, his first few months, he slept four hours at a stretch, no more, and drank 4oz of milk at one go, no more; so with my baby you could plan. He had a bit of trouble with colic but was easy to manage with Infacol; and he had a bit more trouble when his first teeth were on the way. After the first two teeth appeared with all the drama and distress, the next eighteen appeared as if by magic overnight with no fuss at all. I loved being a mother. I had none of that postnatal tension or stress I had heard about, and I was thankful for that. Ayomide ate well and slept well and so, after about five months, I was ready to return to work.

The magazine-distributors I had worked with before I had Ayomide had relocated to Park Royal in north-west London, which I felt was too far away for me to travel to daily, so I was unemployed for a short while before I settled into a new job. I temped for a while and had a series of short assignments before I got a permanent position in a local primary school in Tottenham. Tope, too, spent a while unemployed as the IT contracting market was quite volatile, and he was in and out of contracts. This meant that, even though I had a steady income, our household income rose and fell with Tope's employment situation. But Tope always encouraged me to spread my wings and go places, and, since I worked in a school, I had most school holidays off. A friend of mine moved from the United States to the UK and lived in Milton Keynes. During my holiday, Tope drove Ayomide and me to her house to spend a few days, not at all minding that we were leaving him at home to fend for himself for the week.

Chapter 7

The Love of My Life

In the summer of 2000, a group of us from the Glory House children's church took a one-week trip to a Christian youth-camp run by Elim Pentecostal Church on the Isle of Wight. It was proper camping, not in hostels or caravans but on fields in tents: hot by day and cold by night, with the most beautiful sparkly stars in the dark night sky I had ever seen in my life. Luckily, we had proper toilet and shower-blocks, a laundry-room with washers and dryers and a large kitchen tent. All the adults were workers, and we looked after and served the children. There were fun activities for them during the day and what you could call a church service every evening. After the service there was fun time once again where the children hung out, had burgers and chips and ran around playing games before all their energy was spent and it was time for bed. On our third night at camp, after the evening service, I was getting Ayomide ready for bed, giving him a quick wash in the large sink in the laundry. I had just put him in his pj's when my phone rang. On answering it, it was Tope. He was at the time working on a contract in Southampton. He said he was just calling to say 'hi' and find out how we were doing. He asked me what I was up to, and I explained that I was in the laundry getting Ayomide ready for bed. While I was still speaking with him, the laundry door opened, and there stood Tope in the doorway with his phone to his ear! It was such a fantastic surprise, and I jumped into his outstretched arms. I must have screamed in my excitement because people came running to see what all the fuss was about! Ayomide too was thrilled to see his dad and wanted to go with him at the end of the one-hour visit Tope had with us.

Shortly after that, Ayomide turned two. We had planned for him to have a birthday-party, but it was around that time that Tope's mother took ill and passed away, and, as it just didn't seem appropriate to be celebrating, we gave it a miss. A few months after Tope's mother passed, Tope himself took ill. He had a sharp pain in his back that he just couldn't shift. None of the over-the-counter pain-killers worked, and, even though I'd massage his back every night, it didn't seem to help. One night, he was in so much pain that I had to call for an ambulance. After some treatment with morphine for the pain, a lot of medical investigation was triggered, and it turned out that he had TB. The doctors reckoned he must have picked it up at work. Ayomide and I had to be tested. We had both had the BCG vaccination, and our tests turned out negative. But my darling Tope had to have an operation and months of medical treatment to be free of the infection. That was indeed a scary time. The love of my life was walking about aided by a walking stick. For months we had no idea what the problem was. At one point after an MRI scan, the doctors even thought it was cancer! I prayed, trusted, hoped and believed for his healing. Through it all Tope promised me that this ailment wouldn't kill him and that he would be healed of it, God had told him. And indeed, he did get better, and all was well again.

In the summer of 2001, my parents came to the UK on holiday. That year they both turned sixty, and my siblings and I decided to organise a joint birthday-party for them. The party took place in south London near my sister's house, which was quite far away from mine.

Ayomide was the star of the show, because at the time he was my parents' only grandchild and I had dressed him up in an outfit very similar to my dad's. Tope organised all the music while I was in charge of the two large birthday-cakes. We all had different roles to play, and in the end it all came together to make a beautiful party. My parents were proud of us all for pulling it off.

The two men in my life were growing older and closer: Tope, my darling husband, and our son Ayomide. My guys loved going out together, just the two of them. They would go to the park, to bowls, to the zoo, shopping; they especially liked going to McDonald's together. Tope loved to take photographs, and this was before the era of mobile phone cameras, but Tope took his Cannon SLR camera with him everywhere he went. He made photographic copies of everywhere he had fun. He promptly took his used-up film reel to Costco to get the photographs printed when he was done. Tope was really a fun-loving people-person. He was warm, friendly, genuine and gentle with everyone. Whether he was at work or at church, his attitude to people was the same. They were made in the image of God, and that meant Tope loved them. It often shocked people when Tope told them out of the blue that he loved them - especially other men! My brother for one freaked out the first time Tope said it to him. Tope was always talking about the agape kind of love, God's love. Tope gave himself selflessly to people. He was always ready to help people and taught me to be a more accommodating Christian. He taught me to make time for others, to stop and listen to what people had to say, whether I was really interested or not. He taught me not to judge others, always to realise there was a back-story to everyone's current situation and to accept people and meet them where they were. We had lots of fun in those early days, too. Although we didn't have enough money to go on exotic holidays abroad, we made the most of what we had here in the UK. Once we went to Manchester for a long weekend. It wasn't a birthday or anniversary. We just went for a time-out period, to leave the stress of London behind. We went by coach, which was tight and uncomfortable: I vowed never to travel by coach again. We stayed in a small bed-and-breakfast and did the tourist thing by touring the whole city. It really was fun. Manchester had trams that we didn't have in London and the Trafford Centre (a shopping and entertainment complex built in the shape of a great ship). It was lovely. It had all the high-street shops, every eating joint you could think of and a state-of-the-art cinema. We arrived in Manchester on a Friday night and left on Sunday: a wonderful weekend! On another occasion, we did it with our friends: two other couples, Tope and I. We took ourselves off to a hotel in Crawley for a weekend. We didn't really go out of the hotel but enjoyed each other's company and all the facilities the hotel had to offer: the swimming-pool, gym, restaurant and shops. Every time we had an opportunity to go away for a weekend, we did. We even spent one Valentine's weekend in a Premier Inn down the road from where we lived!

In 2003, after a lot of planning, I fell pregnant with my second child, and once again I experienced all-day sickness not just morning sickness. Again, I was dehydrated and admitted to hospital. The difference was, this time, I had a four-year-old son to worry about, so when I was detained in hospital after an antenatal check-up, I was quite panicked. Tope worked shifts and wasn't always available in the evenings. And it was a constant struggle to get someone to look after my boy when I was suddenly admitted into hospital and put on a drip. This happened four times in the early months of my pregnancy. Tope did amaze me, though, by keeping our flat spotlessly clean while I was in hospital. I would get back home, and even my bathroom would be sparkling clean. When I asked him why he didn't indulge in this level of cleaning when I was not in hospital, he replied that I never let him! I was so impressed by his skills that I nicknamed him my Superman. He often had to sort Ayomide out as well: get him ready for nursery and make his packed lunch. He really was a busy daddy in those first four months.

We were coming up to the end of summer, and, even though I was only about twenty-seven weeks pregnant, I had began to start feeling normal again. We decided to take a week's family trip to Blackpool. We went with another family, our close friends, the Akinsolas. We had a fantastic time. We stayed in a self-catering apartment. The weather was still warm, the beach grand and Blackpool fair phenomenal. We returned shortly before school was to resume in September. Tope went back to work after his short break, and I resumed work in school. Tope was working the night shifts at GMTV that first week of work, and so we didn't see much of each other. However, we had long chats over the phone before I went to bed. Tope told me how proud he was to have a wife like me, seeing that I hadn't given him the cold shoulder or third degree when he told me about the debt he had incurred when he was out of work, as he had informed me over the one-week holiday to Blackpool. We had had enough time to talk candidly about serious issues, and he told me all about his exact financial position, how much our rent was, how much council-tax was, how much he paid on utility bills and how much he paid to credit cards. Before this trip and discussion, I had no idea. The figures were astronomical and took my breath away, but I knew Tope was being transparent with me and laying things bare before me. He didn't have to, and I felt his vulnerability. I swallowed hard and responded that I was glad he had shared this information with me and that together we would work hard and start paying off the debt bit by bit. After all a big portion of the debt was incurred by all our household bills that Tope has insisted he would continue to pay whether he was working or not. He declared his deep love for me and promised to sort out the debt and continue to keep me happy. I went to bed with my heart overflowing with the warmth of love and a smile on my face. Tope came home in the morning and drove me to work before he came back home and took a long nap. By the time I got home that evening, Tope had once again left home and gone to work. Around 10pm when I was getting ready for bed, I called Tope to have a chat, but this time he was busy at work and couldn't have an extensive chat with me like the night before. I said goodnight, and he promised to see me in the morning.

Chapter 8

My Heart is Broken

The morning never came.

I woke up around 5.30am and got myself and Ayomide ready for school. Tope would normally get in around 6am and drive us to school at around 7am. Ayomide and I were ready long before 7am, but Tope didn't turn up. After numerous phone calls and no answer from Tope, I decided to take a bus. We left home around 7.30am. On getting to the office and getting into the swing of things, work got very busy. Before I knew it, it was about 10am, and I still hadn't heard from Tope. This was unusual. Tope should have called me by now. I called his phone, and again it went to voicemail. I decided I would call every hour on the hour till he answered me. I called at 11: no response; again at noon:

still no response. My emotions went from irritation to annoyance and then to panic. I thought something had to be wrong, or why wouldn't Tope have called me? I thought of every scenario that would explain why he hadn't gotten back to me, but none of them made sense. By the end of the day I was convinced something bad had happened. I left work at around 5pm, picked up Ayomide from the childminder and was walking towards the train-station when I got a call. I picked it up quickly, hoping it was at last Tope making contact. 'Hello!', I shouted down the phone. A soft and hesitant voice asked whether I was Mrs Talabi, to which I answered, 'Yes, I am'. He said he was from the Metropolitan Transport Police and wanted to discuss some details of my husband's car with me. I promptly told him I had no interest in discussing his car, only my husband himself. Where is he, I asked? There was a long pause, after which he asked me where I was and said he would send a car to pick me up and would then explain everything. The police-car appeared within a few minutes, and a lady officer got out. She asked me to get in. I refused. I asked her where my husband was. She said she didn't know and that she and her partner had just been instructed to pick me up. I told her I wouldn't go with her until I knew where my husband was. She made a quick phone-call then returned to me. I asked her point-blank, 'Is my husband alive?' She shook her head. I followed her, stunned, holding tightly on to my son's hand. He was only four years old and would never see his dad again. I was thirty-three years old, and today would mark the beginning of a different life for me. So many thoughts were running through my head at great speed. My heart was pounding loudly in my chest and I felt slightly dizzy. I got into the car in a daze and asked the officer again, 'Did you say my husband was dead?' 'Yes', she said but added that she didn't really know the details of the case. All she did know was that Tope had been killed in a road traffic accident at around 6.30am. I brought out my phone with shaky hands and called my friend Funmi (we had gone to Blackpool together). I told her what the police had told me and asked her to meet me at home.

On getting near the house, I started to shake. I really did not want to go indoors, as somehow that made it seem all real. But going into the house was inevitable after all: I couldn't stay in the police-car indefinitely. We lived on the tenth floor of a tower-block, and we had to take the lift. As I listened to the screeching of the lift-cables carrying us up to the tenth floor, I felt as if I was going to explode, struggling to hold it all in (not sure why). At the tenth floor, the doors slowly opened, and Funmi was waiting for me just outside my front door. I gave her my keys, and she opened the door. As I stepped in with Ayomide by my side and the police at my heels, I saw one foot of Tope's sandals by the bedroom door, and the flood-gates burst open. I started to cry, quietly at first, but, before I knew it, I was screaming. I kept on asking, what I was going to do now? how was I going to carry on without the love of my life? I didn't want to carry on, I wanted to close my eyes and die too. How could Tope have left me to carry on without him? This was not fair, I cannot do it, I will not do it, I refuse to carry on! This was all the madness spewing out of my mouth as the tears flowed uncontrollably down my face. Funmi held me and tried to console me, but the truth was she was grief-stricken as well; it was all just a horrible experience. The police waited while I calmed down and then asked me loads of questions, I cannot remember what, but between us Funmi and I answered all their questions. Shortly after the police left, people started to arrive: my pastors, my two brothers, my sister and my sister-in-law, Tope's brother, his brother's wife and his sister. In a short while, the little flat was full of people, all at different stages of acceptance. It was such a shock that someone so full of life as Tope could now suddenly be dead. Above all emotions, I was bewildered. I just couldn't imagine how I was going to carry on living without Tope. I just kept on asking what I was going to do. I remember at one point my brother, Timi, hugged me really tightly and whispered in my ear that everything was going to be all right. I believed him, and for the next twenty minutes I thought I'd be okay. I spent that night with Funmi and her husband Akin. My sister, Tinu, stayed with me as well. I had a very rough night: I kept on waking up and realising that Tope was really dead and it wasn't just a nightmare. The visitors continued to arrive, everyone that knew us wanted to pay their respects. I think the fact that I was heavily pregnant as well made me a bit of an enigma, and people were curious to come and see how I was coping with the situation. After a couple of nights, I began to reset my mind. okay, so now I'm a widow, I have a four-year-old son that needs me; I also have a baby on the way that needs me. These two lives, for which I was now solely responsible, were reason enough for me to carry on. I began to consider the things I must do to make carrying on possible. I knew I had to accept that Tope had gone, that I would never see him again, that I would never again feel his touch or feel his breath in my ear as he whispered he loved me. I had to accept that I no longer had the support of one that loved and believed in me even more than I believed in myself. Truly, I was now on my own. I had never been a good sharer, generally keeping myself to myself and never in the habit of sharing my hopes, concerns, dreams or desires with anyone except Tope. I turned to God. God, how am I going to walk this journey without my darling Tope? God, I really need to hear from you, otherwise I'm groping around in the dark, lost and disoriented. As always, the Lord hears me when I call. His word says, 'Seek and you will find, knock and the door will be opened to you.' God sent his word to me, in the early days while I was having a quiet moment in his presence. These were his words to me:

No temptation has overtaken you except such as is common to man; but God is faithful, who will not allow you to be tempted beyond what you are able, but with the temptation will also make the way of escape, that you may be able to bear it. **1 Corinthians 10:13**.

This word to me meant that I could actually weather this storm! I would not lose my mind to grief, because God's word to me promised that I would not be tempted beyond what I was able to bear. This became my mantra. I used to mutter it to myself over and over. I had to believe it, to live it. So, from around day three, I pulled myself together and decided to hold my head high. After all, Tope died and went to heaven, God is not dead and he would help me carry on. I had my tearful moments, but they were usually in the privacy of my bedroom.

Chapter 9

It's Dark, Will the Sunshine Return?

My mother arrived about a week after Tope's death, and, as soon as I saw her, all my built-up strength disappeared, and I broke down in tears. It was the biggest melt down I had had since the one I had on the day Tope died. My mother held me in her arms, and I sobbed. This release actually made me feel much better. My mother was here now to take the reins and be in charge of everyday things; even help me look after Ayomide, cook, clean and make sure everything was in order. This was a great relief.

The funeral was imminent, in just a few days' time. I had been to the funeral directors and chosen a casket and a plot of land which Tope's employers, GMTV, had graciously paid for. My church, Glory House, had also given me a lump sum of money towards the funeral. On the day, I took a ride from the T. Cribbs Funeral Home in Beckton, in a shiny black limousine with Ayomide by my side, in a convoy with three other black shiny cars along with the hearse. We slowly pulled into Tabernacle Avenue, where my church was. The main auditorium was already full of congregants and mourners. As I walked through the aisle to the front-row seat, I had this feeling of dread and finality. The casket was a few yards in front of me, opened for mourners to pay their last respects. In it lay my Tope, although he looked as if he were just asleep; stone cold and hard to the touch. Life had indeed left this body. The corpse lying there before me was not really my Tope any more. He had truly gone, left this world forever. I felt bereft all over again.

After the funeral, my life post-Tope began. At first, my new reality was surreal. I kept on wondering why life seemed to be going on as normal: did life not know my husband had died? Everyone and everything around me just carried on as if nothing had happened; truly life just went on. I had to handle all the administration of Tope's affairs. He had no assets but credit cards, bank accounts, Telewest broadband, T-Mobile phone service, BT land-line, Enfield council-house rent and council-tax, to mention a few. I spent a lot of time making phone-calls, sending e-mails and even posting hard-copy letters, as was common in those days. Ayomide returned to school, but I stayed at home and started my maternity leave earlier than I would have. A friend had offered to take Ayomide to school, and she did so for the first couple of weeks. Every morning, Ayomide would cling to me and cry that he didn't want to go to school. He was only four years old and in reception class, and I realised that it wasn't that he didn't want to go to school: he was more worried that I might disappear as his dad had. I had to understand and accept that it wasn't only me going through a bereavement. My son, young though he was, was going through his own trauma as well. I tried my best to reassure him that I wasn't going anywhere, and it took him a while to be okay away from me. I too was struggling with my own demons. I was terrified of being a single mother. I had grown up in a close family, where my both parents had been present to shape and mould my life. I didn't leave home till I was twenty-four years old, and in all those years I had the covering of both my parents.

One Saturday morning, I woke up in a bit of a panic. I was worried about bringing up my son on my own without a father. I lay there on my bed, pondering and eventually working myself up into a state of hysteria. Once again, God came to the rescue over the telephone. My phone rang, and it was my brother Timi. I told him how scared I was about being a single mother to my son. He immediately reminded me that Tope had testified at a men's meeting about a year before how he had been brought up by a single mother and had made the decision to choose God as his father. My brother asked me, 'Didn't he turn out fine?' When I responded, 'Yes', he said, 'Your son will be fine, too'. This quenched the panic in my soul.

It was about four weeks after Tope died, when I had my first dream about him. My dreams always consist of what's on my mind, and, as Tope was always on my mind, I was a bit perplexed that I hadn't dreamt about him earlier. Anyway, finally it happened. In the dream I was in a big crowd of people. It could have been in church or in a house-church group. I saw Tope in the distance. He was wearing a most unlikely attire: white shirt and white trousers with a yellow tank-top. I was sitting on a short wall when I spotted him in the distance. As soon as I saw him, I jumped down from the wall and ran towards him. As I reached him and tried to fling my arms around him, he stopped me. He said I couldn't touch him yet. He pulled out his phone and his wallet from his pockets and gave them to me. 'These are yours now, keep them,' he said. There was a bit more to the dream, but that's all I remembered. I had other vivid dreams of Tope, some serious and some quite playful, and till this day, every now and again, Tope pops up in my dreams as if to take his rightful place in my heart. Shortly after my first dream of Tope, GMTV, the company Tope had worked for, got in touch with me and paid out a lump sum to me as a kind of insurance pay-out. I used this money to buy a flat which I rented out so I could make the monthly mortgage repayments.

I returned to church about six weeks after Tope's passing. Sitting in the pews without Tope by my side was akin to torture. It just wasn't right. No matter who sat next to me, it felt wrong. But I soon learnt how to put on a pretty smile and smile through the agony. Some worship songs made my smile wobble, or particular references from the pulpit also caused me a bit of grief, but, on the whole, I managed okay. One Sunday morning, I received a message, written on a small piece of paper, passed to me through the aisles. A lady, whom I did not know, the mother of the wife of a friend, had sent me a message to say, 'Those tears that you shed every morning when you first get up must now come to an end. Enough of it', the note said. No one but God witnessed those tears. They happened as I opened my eyes every morning and realised that Tope was still dead. Not even my kids saw them. I would weep for a few minutes and then pull myself together and start my day. Now I was being instructed to stop it. I was not doing it on purpose, but, from then on, the tears dried up. The deep intense sadness and sense of loss, however, took much longer to subside. Tope had an uncle who, when Tope was alive, used to call me 'Iyawo Ijebu', a pet name which meant I was their village bride. The first time I spoke to him after Tope had died and he called me Tara, I wept. My loss had even stripped me of that title. It was a silly little thing, and I know Uncle K meant me no harm. He couldn't call me a bride when the groom was no more, but the pain cut deep, and it was one more emotion I had to tuck away somewhere out of sight.

Chapter 10

Tom Sawyer was his Nickname

Tomi is my second brother, the younger of my two brothers. He was nicknamed Tom Sawyer as a child because he often got into scrapes similar to Tom Sawyer's in the *Huckleberry Finn* stories. If you meet him today and wonder what the origin of his name Sawyer was, well, that's the story behind it. When Tope died, Tomi was an undergrad in Middlesex University, and his halls of residence were in Tottenham. This meant that, geographically, he was the nearest to me of my three siblings, and he was the first of them to arrive on the scene. He stayed very close to me and ran every errand for me. He was at my beck and call and eventually moved in with me. His presence made home feel cosy. There was me, Ayomide, my mother and Tomi living together. Tomi drove me to Sainsbury's on

Saturday, where I did my weekly shopping, and to church on Sunday for weekly service. And he took me everywhere else I needed to be in between.

My first Christmas without Tope was approaching quickly, and my siblings rallied around to make it great. I had just moved out of the flat Tope and I had shared into a three-bedroomed house down the road. My brother Timi and his family spent a few days with me over Christmas, so did my sister Tinu. I had all my siblings and my mother with me for that first Christmas. It made Tope's absence bearable. In fact, because I was in a different house, it felt as if I was on holiday away from home. I was due to have my baby in the first week of January. On the last Sunday of the year, after service, someone came to me and said there was someone looking for me in the sports-hall. As I pushed open the doors to the sports-hall and stepped inside, there was a loud shout of surprise! My friends and family in church had organised a baby shower for me. There was food and drinks and loads of baby gifts. I didn't know whether to laugh or cry.

As the days approached, I was ready for my baby's arrival. I had my bags packed, but the baby didn't seem to be in a hurry to arrive. Every twitch set me on edge but ultimately turned out to be a false alarm. At forty weeks and six days, I was invited to come into the hospital to be induced. My brother, Tomi took me in on a Sunday night. The procedure was scheduled for early the next morning. In the middle of the night, my contractions started. My daughter was born at 8am on 13 January 2004. She was a most welcome baby: a girl! Now I was complete. I had a son and a daughter, I felt as if I had no need to be married, God had given me what I wanted, a baby girl. But the journey of single motherhood seemed to have just begun: a season wherein I had to make all the decisions regarding two little lives on my own. Thank God, my mother was present, even my brother and sister were present, but ultimately I was solely responsible for my two children.

Aramide Oluwaremilekun Modurotoluwa Isabelle Talabi was a loud baby! She did everything with vigour. She was nothing like her brother. Ayomide and I had to adjust our expectations to accommodate her. When we got home from the hospital, Aramide slept for twelve hours straight on her first night at home. When I woke up in the morning, I sat and watched her sleep, I poked her to make sure she was still breathing. She just squeezed her face and carried on sleeping. I remember going to the bathroom, and, when I got back, Ayomide was sitting on a chair in my room with his baby sister in his arms. I was about to scream but thought I shouldn't startle him in case he dropped her.

He said he loved his sister and was going to marry her. Still she slept through it all. When she eventually woke up, she made a very loud cry like someone had pinched her, but she was really just announcing that she was awake now.

During this period of my life, I was surrounded with so much love and support that I really couldn't complain. I had time to recover and heal. I could choose to be quiet and remain behind closed doors or come out of my room and enjoy the company of my family and friends that stayed very close to me. Funmi and Akin visited me every day for the first month after Tope died. Toyin and Dipo took over after they stopped and visited me every Friday night once Aramide was born. My sister Tinu spent every weekend with me for a whole year. She would arrive on Friday and go back to her home on Sunday. My mother, after staying with me for six months, went back to Nigeria for a couple of months and then returned with my father, both staying with me for another six months. At some point, I thought Aramide didn't really know who I was, as she had so many loved ones looking after her. Dipo and some other close friends of Tope organised friends and family to make a monthly standing-order donation to my account for as long as they were comfortable doing it. It was amazing. People gave so much, either as a one-off donation or as a standing order. Sometimes I even had cash arrive anonymously in the post. In those early days those standing orders added up to over £900 a month! For years the standing orders continued, even though they dwindled year on year. I was grateful to God for the lives of everyone that sowed into my life. It just meant that money was never a problem, and I could pay back debts like outstanding council-tax bills without its being a financial strain. There were lots of blessings. Some people still give me a standing order to this day. A friend of my sister, Ade, sends me a bag of rice every Christmas. She continues to do so to this day. Another friend of mine from church, Mummy Hallelujah and her husband deliver to me periodically an array of foodstuffs: rice, oil, chicken, fish etc. She continues to do this to this to this day. I cannot document all the generosity to me from people over the years. There have been so many blessings. The Lord knows them all and will reward their kindness.

I needed to learn how to drive, and once again God sent favour my way. A good friend, Bukki Jamo, made it her mission to see me pass my driving test. I eventually got my licence in August 2004, and finally my brother Tomi was free of chauffeur duties. He rejoiced, and I thought he was just so happy for me, but the truth was, he had his life back. He could now come and go as he pleased because he was no longer responsible for getting me from point A to B. It wasn't quite one year that Tope left, but the training wheels of my existence were coming off, and I was quickly learning the art of independence.

Chapter 11

Returning to Work

In April 2004, I went back to work. Aramide was only three months old, but, as I had started my maternity leave months earlier than I would have, I felt I had been at home for long enough. My first challenge on returning to work was my computer's operating system. Before I went on leave, I had been using Microsoft XP for over a year. On my return, it had changed to Windows 7. Any computer problems I had, my first call was always to Tope. On my second day back at work, trying to find my way around Windows 7, I stretched out my hand to pick up my work-phone to call Tope and ask him for help. As I touched the receiver, I remembered my situation, and it was like a stab in my heart. Of course, my eyes welled up with tears, but I had to hold it together; after all, I was at work and determined to be professional. I now had to call the IT support first provided by the council for all my tech support, but being back at work was a good thing. It gave me something other than my loss to focus on. I focused on work and on being a great mother. My two children were young and needed me for everything, so I made my life about theirs. My whole existence was mummy, work and church. I didn't have much time or energy for social activities outside this triangle. I had a few invitations to go to places where children were not invited, and I just felt that the people that invited me to such places were very ill informed. I gladly turned down those invitations, stating that, if my children were not welcome, neither was I, and for those who protested too loudly, I asked them to provide me with child-care, and that soon shut them up. As I loved having my children around me and didn't want them out of my sight, I tried to discourage sleep-overs with friends as much as possible.

In December 2004, I took the children home to Nigeria for Christmas. Going home to my parents was just wonderful. The children and I were all pampered and doted on for the whole of our stay. The children thought their grandparents' house was a mansion, as it was the biggest house they had ever seen. They were introduced to the legendary mosquitos which took delight in biting them all over. But on the whole we had a brilliant two weeks before we had to return to the UK. On landing at London Heathrow, I started experiencing ulcer pains, which were brought on by the stress of knowing that I was back in charge and responsible for life. Back in Nigeria, I had no care in the world, everything was done for me and taken care of. It was very relaxing to let go of the reins. But back home in London, I had to call all the shots. In March of 2005 we boarded a plane again. This time, Tope's brother Bola and his wife Abbey took us on holiday to their home in Orlando, Florida. We spent ten days enjoying the Disney parks and the company of family. The following year, we went to Rome with our friends Toyin and Dipo. We also went with them to Malaga in Spain. Some other time we went to South Dakota to visit my friend Deola and her family. It's amazing to remember that I went to all these places when I'd much rather stay in my own home, as I'm not really fond of globetrotting. I am glad, however, that my children got to go places, because, if it was just up to me, they probably wouldn't have left the country. A big thank you to all my family and friends that made holidays happen for the children and me!

In 2006, when Ayomide turned seven, I decided to have a big birthday-party for him. It was football themed. I invited his whole year group from school and friends and family from church. There were about seventy children in all. Surprisingly, Ayomide did not relish the attention. He was fine with the running around and playing football but miserable when he had to smile and cut the cake. He just detested all the attention. That was the last big celebration he's had. It was clear that he just was not one for all that kind of festivity.

Chapter 12

Being a Solo Mum

Aramide was soon to start nursery, and I had to warn the staff not to expect another Ayomide, because Aramide was very different from her brother. Even though she was only three years old, she was opinionated, feisty and quite bossy. Her first day in nursery, she hadn't yet learnt to spell her own name, but she took it upon herself to show all the other children how to spell theirs. She loved the nursery and her teachers and was eager to leave the house every morning.

Ayomide was now in Year 3, the second half of primary school. I used to drop them both off at their childminder as early as 7.20am Monday to Friday and pick them up when I left work after 5pm. By the time we got home after school, it was usually around 6pm. It was then dinner, homework and bed-time. By 9pm, I was shattered and had it for the day. The cycle continued the next day until the weekend, when I had a slight breather in the form of a lie-in, but then I had ten sets of uniforms to wash and iron ready for the next week. Sunday was church and relaxation for the rest of the day. This was my life for the next few years; nothing too interesting ever happened. I looked after my children, went to work and went to church. That was it. I kept a low profile everywhere I was. I kept my wedding-rings on because I didn't want anyone to think I was available to be a girl-friend, mistress or wife. I had zero desire for such complications in my life. Friends and family would ask when I would consider getting into a new relationship, and my answer to this day remains the same: I already seemed to have had the best there was to have. Tope fulfilled all my dreams and, since he continues to populate my dreams every now and again, there seemed to be no room at all for someone else. Besides, I loved Tope with such abandon, and I'd loathe to do that again. I will always be cautious, not to love too hard because there is the possibility of loss. I have heard that to love and lose is better than never to have loved at all. But to love and lose a second or third time would be very bad for the soul, I happily maintained my lane as a single person.

About five years after Tope had gone, I began to feel restless. I should have been over the loss by now and begun to feel better. I wasn't feeling better, but everyone else had moved on. I had by now met people who knew nothing about my history, who I felt wouldn't understand what my life was about. It was almost as if I had held down my grief for so long and it was now determined to come bubbling up to the surface. When I saw couples together, I would feel a stab of jealousy in my heart. Jealousy is a horrible feeling, but I couldn't switch it off.

All I wanted was to be happily married, but somehow that wasn't my portion. One day, at work, I came across a leaflet advertising EDF Energy. On it was the picture of a family, father, mother, son and daughter, all sitting together on a sofa in a living-room. I took one look at it and burst into tears. The rush of emotion came totally out of the blue; I was devastated. I wanted to be the mother in the leaflet, sitting with my husband and children in the living-room. Luckily, I was alone in my office when this happened. I began to think I might need to speak to someone, some sort of counsellor who could help me sort out the pain in my heart. I toyed with the idea of a Christian counsellor or even a secular one, but none presented themselves at that time. I prayed about it and decided all I needed to do was to talk to someone I trusted and just get it off my chest. My hesitation was that most people I knew had moved on, and I feared they wouldn't understand why I was so disturbed this length of time after the event. This was a further reason why I bottled it all up. Eventually, I decided to write an email to my friend Funmi. I downloaded all the rumblings in my heart. I told her all. I also told her not to visit me. All I needed her to do was to pray for me, from her house and not in mine. I was too embarrassed to face her after baring my soul like that. When I was done, I felt a physical release, as if I had really set down some heavy luggage I was carrying. I still hadn't recovered from the embarrassment I felt when I saw Funmi in Church on Sunday. I hid myself. I felt as if my protective cloak had been stripped off me. Now Funmi could see me down to my soul. I didn't like it. But I liked the fact that I could sleep better after baring all to her in my email, so I just had to deal with it. Funmi hugged me and said all would be well, and actually all was well.

Another part I found hard over the years was the role of a single mother. Please be assured, my children are my pride and joy; my love for them kept me alive when I wanted to die; but life was just easier with Tope by my side. He had a very positive spin on life, making even hard things seem simple. I have done and continue to do my best, but there is always room for improvement. Having to make decisions for the children without running it past another person or just discussing it to bring to an ultimate agreed end I found very hard. I found it hard that my children could only ask me for stuff and not turn around and ask their dad if I refused. That there's no dad on hand to show my son the ropes, to show him how to handle a power tool or just how to be a man was hard for me. And that there is no daddy to take my daughter on her first date or walk her down the aisle when she gets married makes me feel a little bit sad. In my opinion, parenting is not a one-person job. It's a hard task even for two active parents. For one parent, it's extra tricky. But for God's grace, I could have messed everything up. I saw the places where I was weak and wished I wasn't doing the journey alone. But I didn't have the energy, capacity or desire to replace Tope, no matter how challenging I found the job of a single mother. But I shrug it off and continue my journey, because pondering these things is not really productive.

When Aramide was five, she had a big birthday-party. She glowed in all the attention and had a great time. All her friends from school and church were present, and they all seemed delighted with their party-bags at the end of the day. My friend Joke had come to the UK to do her wedding shopping and was present at the party too, which made the day extra special for me. It was 2009, and I had to go to Nigeria for a few days to attend Joke's wedding. Ayomide stayed at home with my brother Tomi while Aramide stayed with my friend and colleague Jennifer. It was my shortest trip to Nigeria but I'm glad I went.

My dad pampered me over the few days I was at home, and I remember the trip with extra fond memories as this was the last time I saw my father, because he died a year later after a brief illness. He was a contradiction of sorts. He was a fierce and formidable darling: a big hard man on the outside but really not so hard on the inside. His emotions ran quick and deep, so he loved passionately and fiercely, but he also had the quickest and hottest temper I know. He was a very jolly fellow, he was witty and you could crack your ribs laughing at his jokes. He certainly was a bit of a contradiction. He was born precious. He was his parents' fourth child, but their first son, this made him very special indeed, so he grew up very pampered and privileged. Then he married my mother, and she continued to pamper him till his last breath.

In life, he always had his way because no one actually dared defy him, not at home and not even at work. At home, everything was done for him. I'm not sure he could even boil an egg. That was not his calling as a husband and father. His was to provide financially and to maintain the cars and household electronics, which he did with diligence. When I was growing up, if we were really naughty, he was called to inflict punishment and maintain discipline. This was never a good thing, because a spanking from my dad was never in moderation. But he loved us, his children, fiercely, although he was not very good at showing it. However, we all knew we were well loved, and it was no secret that I was his favourite child! I was his first creation. I looked like him, I was well mannered and had a beautiful temperament and was good in school. I, in turn, glowed in his love. I was secure in the fact that he was always proud of me. Even as an adult, my dad used to look at me as if I was his best creation. His passing therefore made me feel even more bereft, because I knew the relationship I had with him could not be replaced.

In fewer than ten years, I had lost my husband and then my father. Why were the men in my life deserting me so prematurely? Both my parents were over fifty before they lost their parents, but I guess our destinies are different. Mine seemed to be to stand alone without the support of a man. From the beginning of 2010, friends and family had asked what I would be doing to celebrate my fortieth birthday, but I had no plan. Despite the fact that I loved to plan way in advance, I somehow found it difficult to plan for my fortieth. In February, I still had no plan for my birthday in August. So when my father passed away in April, it made sense that a big party in August would never have worked for me. All my siblings and their families and I went to Nigeria to bury my father. All my mother's children and grandchildren turned up from the UK, her assets all in one basket. We were looked after like precious goods. The funeral was a grand affair, and, even though we went to Nigeria for something that was essentially sad, it was really nice to be away from home with my siblings and nephews and niece, all under one roof. It was as if we were on a holiday with a mission. But, like all things that have a beginning, the end came ever so quickly, and we all had to return to real life in the UK. Leaving my mother on her own in Nigeria without my dad felt strange, but we were making plans for her next visit to the UK as soon as possible.

I did eventually go ahead and plan my fortieth birthday-party when I returned home. It was late summer of 2010, and it was a house-party instead of one in an events-hall. Most of my friends and family attended. The house was full inside and out; guests were even spilling out into the car-park. There was all manner of food available, and a barbecue was set up in the garden. Everyone that wanted to attend turned up, and there was more than enough food, drink and music to keep everyone merry.

At forty I decided to take a closer look at my career. Both my children were a bit older and less dependent, so I decided to take some courses to enhance my career development. I had been ten years in my current job, and it was a good time for me to take stock. I remembered that I started out as an administrative officer of the lower half of a school, but, over the years, like most things, the job evolved, and my responsibilities grew. It came to a point where I could no longer just switch off from work at the end of the day and forget all till the next day. With more responsibility comes more accountability, which means more vigilance and more work. By 2011 I was doing many more hours at work, and I had become responsible for the administration not only of the lower school but for the upper school as well. Somewhere along the way, my job-title had changed to School Business Manager and, along with that, my duties, responsibilities and remuneration had changed also. On my journey to this point, I had done some courses just to familiarise myself with IT in the work-place and computer software that would help me at work. As I found both courses on the internet and they were run fully online, I knew these kinds of courses existed. Again, I looked for courses more suited to what I was doing daily. The first one I found was a certificate in school business administration. Shortly after that, I did another diploma in school office efficiency. These kept me busy for most evenings. I would take the kids to swimming lessons and sit in the car and do my work. In those days I was mummy-cum-chauffeuse. It was one after-school activity after the other, and I was mostly driving back and forth from one activity or another: if it wasn't swimming, it was karate or football or drama class or after-school study-classes. We even did a weekend reading-school. I did my best to broaden the children's horizon as far as I could within my comfort zone. I made sure they attended every single school trip and residential course offered them, and that covered all the national museums, amusement parks and local theatres; this to me was a big part of their education.

Chapter 13

My Darling Mother

One of the biggest challenges I experienced during my early forties was watching my mother's health deteriorate. It was Christmas of 2011, and my mother was at home in Lagos, and she had told me she was going to Ijebu Ode to spend Christmas with her sister. I also was planning to spend Christmas at home with my brothers and sisters here in London. That year, everyone was coming to mine, and we planned to have a great time. My mother was scheduled to travel on 22 December. I received a phone-call that evening, informing me that she had been involved in a road traffic accident on her way to Ijebu Ode. During the accident some items in the car that were not securely fastened down had been dislodged and hit her in the back. As this caused her some level of internal bleeding and a perforated stomach, she had to be rushed to a teaching hospital, out of state, for an emergency operation. I received the message but was unable to speak with her. All this happened a few days before Christmas. I was, however, assured by my mother's sister, that she was receiving treatment and responding well. It put a little bit of a damper on Christmas, but the fact that I was with my siblings and their families made the time bearable. A couple of days after Christmas, my mother was now post-operation, and she had started receiving visitors in hospital. One of her visitors, my cousin, phoned me while he was with my mother and allowed me to speak with her. It was such a relief to hear her on the phone, and I remember breaking down in tears. It's a very fragile existence when you are staying strong; a slight bit of nice can just undo all your strength. I was so relieved to hear her voice, strong and peculiar. She had a unique voice: no one sounded quite like her, and, at that moment, her voice was music to my ears.

The procedure revealed other health complications that we were unaware of previously. My mother had stage-four breast cancer that had metastasised to her bones; but she was alive. The accident had not killed her. The operation to repair her perforated stomach caused by the car accident was a success, but we were informed she would need treatment for the cancer. My siblings and I all reside in the UK, and we decided the best course of action was to bring her to the UK to start treatment. I needed a Nigerian visa or Nigerian passport to make the trip. I had neither. A visa was easier to get at the time, but I needed a letter of invitation from someone in Nigeria and a number of supporting documents to make the application complete. My cousin Afolabi came to my rescue. He provided me with all his personal documents that I needed for the visa. This was a great help indeed and made the process quite straightforward.

About six weeks after my mother's operation, I travelled to Nigeria in February 2012 to collect her and bring her back to the UK with me. On getting to Nigeria, Afolabi picked me up from the airport and immediately booked an appointment for me with the Nigerian passport-office for me to get a Nigerian passport before I returned to the UK. I travelled to Ibadan to pick up my mother, who had been discharged into the care of my aunty, Mrs Osunkoya, and we returned to Lagos to pack up for our trip back to the UK. My parents' home in Isolo Lagos had been locked up since my mother had been in hospital. On reaching the house, we discovered that the house had been burgled and my mother's bedroom totally ransacked. Jewellery and cash had been stolen, and, even though there were foot-prints and finger-prints all over the place, that part of Lagos was not one where forensic evidence would hold any water. The police in this matter would be as efficient as a chocolate teapot! We tidied everything up and started to pack up for our journey. In the mean time I attended my appointment at the passport-office and came home with my Nigerian passport. You can accomplish almost anything in Nigeria if you have the right connections and enough money. In a few days we were back on a Virgin flight, landing at London Heathrow.

My brother Timi picked us up and drove us to my sister's house, where my mother was going to stay. Shortly after we arrived, my mother saw her GP, who in turn referred her to a specialist. After many tests, the diagnosis from Nigeria was confirmed, and it was advised that the disease was so advanced that palliative care was the only way forward. Over the next few months, my mother was recovering nicely from her operation. Her good friend Dr Cole had prescribed her a very healthy herbal diet, which helped to speed up her recovery and slow down the degenerative process of the cancer. As soon as she was strong enough, she returned to church and attended religiously at least twice a week.

My siblings and I had agreed that if my mother was to stay with us here in the UK we needed to regularize her immigration status and get her an indefinite right to remain in the country. We gathered all the necessary papers, got a lawyer and made the application to the Home Office. All we had to do now was wait.

One evening, my mother turned up on my doorstep. She had come over because she wanted me to take her for a Friday night prayer-vigil in church scheduled for that night. This was an all-night prayer time that we had periodically in church (it started at around midnight and ended around 5am). I told my mother I had no intention of attending on that particular day. I had had a long day at work, gone shopping and was then too tired. My mother refused to have it. She just kept up showing up in my room and telling me how many minutes of rest I had left. Eventually, I got up and grudgingly started to get ready. I told her I wasn't going for the meeting, just taking her there and bringing her back. I picked up a large blanket, a pillow and my car keys and marched downstairs to my car. When we got to church, I found myself a quiet spot, made myself comfortable and had a good sleep. When it was about half an hour to the end of the meeting, I got up, folded my blanket and joined the rest of the congregation praying. Just before the closing prayer, pastor made a declaration. He said that God had told him that everyone that had attended the meeting and had come with a specific petition would receive their miracle within the next seven days. If this was all I came for, I prayed to God that he could leave me out of the equation, but, for the faith my mother had shown, Lord, please give her a miracle. On day six after that meeting, I received a phone call from lawyers informing me that my mother had been granted an indefinite right to remain in the UK. The lawyer said that in her twenty years of working in immigration law, she had never come across a case that happened so swiftly. This was indeed a miracle!

My mother was the strongest woman I knew: a warrior ever ready for battle, be it in the spirit or emotionally, she would rise to the occasion when the time came. Even now that she has passed, I still am yet to come across any woman with her strength of character. She lived with all her strength; she was a go-getter. If she made up her mind that something needed to be done, she would move mountains to make sure it was done. If you were supposed to follow her and were dragging your feet, she would leave you behind and go it alone. She loved passionately, and she was very particular about the difference between right and wrong. My mother was very proper. She believed things had to be done in a certain way, and if they weren't she was not happy. If someone did you a favour or gave you a gift, you said thank you. My mother believed that when you got home or that person got home, you called them up or send them a message again, to say thank you, to show that you truly appreciated and were not just being flippant. She was old-fashioned like that, but her old-fashioned ways endeared her to many and earned respect in many quarters.

Now in my early forties, I had my two young children, progressing well at work, loving and supportive siblings and friends and an aged and ailing mother. I didn't have a dad, and I didn't have a husband to share my deep and most secret concerns. I actually yearned for both my dad, who in his latter years treated me like a princess, and my husband, who had treated me like a diamond emerging from the rough into dazzling brightness. I always held my head high, but I missed being able to lie down at night and download my thoughts and concerns for the day. Tope always knew how to tell me that everything would be all right. He knew the exact prayer to pray with me to boost my faith and confidence and make big issues seem manageable. When I was living with my mother's sickness, even though I had my siblings to share her care and treatment, I still felt lonely in my spirit, often inadequate because I had hardened my heart: I had built a wall around my emotions just so that I could remain composed. This might have made me seem insensitive, but it was all just an act and a defensive mechanism, the only way I knew how to weather the storm of watching my mother dying before my very eyes. She had a couple of years where she had recovered from the operation after her car accident, and she seemed to gain strength and purpose. During that time, she was like a busy bee. She was involved in all sorts of Christian ministry and engaged in some form of activity almost every day of the week. However, her disease was like a lethal time-bomb ticking quietly away in the background.

Chapter 14

The Young are Growing

My boy had reached secondary-school age now, and choosing a secondary school was just another thing in my face highlighting that I was a single mother. I lived in the Borough of Enfield, and neither my borough nor my neighbouring boroughs offered the 11+ exams. For this reason, we didn't have any grammar schools in the area. In church, all my son's mates were preparing for the 11+ exams. They had fancy tutors that cost an arm and a leg, and they were all choosing fancy grammar schools. My son showed no interest in this, and it was fine by me. It meant I didn't have to look for the extra cash to fund the private lessons, didn't have to drive him to and from the lessons, and he wouldn't go to school so far away from home that getting there and back would be an issue. However, I avoided all those parent cliques that were discussing 11+ for fear of being looked down on and so as not to feel inadequate myself. If Tope was alive, he would have gladly ferried the child to a fro, and between us we would have been able to afford to finance the fancy tutors, but on my own it would have been a struggle, and I just had to choose the battles I was willing to have. That's not to say he never had tutors. He had tutors all through secondary school.

Choosing from my local community schools meant that I had a smaller selection to choose from. Choosing a church school seemed to be the way to go, since I worked for one, and my son attended one as his primary school. I chose three schools instead of five. The first had a Christian affiliation and was brand new, with state-of-the-art facilities. The second was a Church of England school in an old derelict building. The third was a Roman Catholic school, one that we had little chance of getting into unless I lied, which I wasn't about to do, so really I had only two choices. After I had submitted the application forms, I spoke with a friend, who then said some things that made me feel that my first choice was probably not the best idea; but, since it was done, I left it as it was. As God would have it, when the offers were published, my boy was offered our second choice - which was just perfect! I was quite excited about his going off to big school, but, like all things in life, every step into the future seems to come with its own set of challenges.

My boy was hardly ever in trouble in primary school, but, come secondary school, I was called on almost weekly for one misdemeanour or another. I quickly realised that the way primary schools looked after their children is very different from the way secondary schools seemed to do it. It takes the children a while to settle into the new way of nurturing. Gone is the motherly nurturing teacher that had probably known the child since he was in nursery. Here comes this teacher whose life's desire is for you to stand still and listen without fidgeting. For a Year 7 child, this is a skill that has to be learned, and they don't all learn it at the same pace. My boy's voice broke very early on in his Year 7, and when he whispered it just sounded like a quiet groan on a microphone. He was always pulled up for talking in class, and I'm certain he was never talking to himself! You were only allowed to be pulled up on so many occasions before your parent got called in. I was called in quite early on in the first term, and this continued numerous times throughout his time in Year 7. I would have to leave work really early, having to reveal to my colleagues at work that my boy had been naughty and his school had summoned me, almost breaking all the driving regulations just to get there on time for my appointment. This made me angry, not for the reasons they called me to his school, because talking in class or flicking his pencil was only a mild annoyance for me, but I was also slightly irritated that I had to leave work early and deal with school-runs traffic. But even more than that, I was angry because I felt that, if his father were alive and had given him a stern warning, his behaviour at school would have been different. I, however, was called back multiple times to address more or less the same issue of his low-level disruption in class.

I grew up in a two-parent home, and what you could do and get away with, with my mum, you certainly couldn't with my dad. I attended my son's school so many times that the school started to suggest that the reason my son was naughty was because his dad had died when he was young. Now even though I thought this was ridiculous, I allowed them to make excuses for my boy's behaviour if it made them feel useful. They suggested he might need some pastoral care, which I agreed to, but it turned out he just needed to pay more attention in class and stop distracting the other kids. He was a well-balanced lovely boy who just got easily bored by hard work. What's new?

By this time, my daughter was in Year 2. Aramide Isabelle Talabi was sent to this world to challenge me and keep me awake. From a very young age, she was feisty and opinionated. The best way to imagine her personality and attitude to life is to think of her like a can of coke. She has an effervescent nature. She is bubbly, loud and has a tremendous amount of stuff to say. Now anyone who knows me will know I am the exact opposite of my baby. I'm not what you would call quiet, but I am certainly on the reserved side and a bit more pessimistic than optimistic. Aramide is forever optimistic. To her, everything is doable; she has big dreams, and, to her, they are all totally realistic. It's no wonder that a child like this was constantly in trouble. Her troubles were that she couldn't shut up. She argued with everyone to get her own opinion across. She was always busy doing her own thing and resented having to stop what she was doing to do what someone else wanted her to do, so she clashed with her teachers because she always had something to say even when she was supposed to stay quiet. After all the observations and psychoanalysis around behavioural issues, it turned out that my daughter just wanted or required more of me than I was giving her. Remember, I am on the reserved side, and she is certainly not. But I had to learn to come out of my comfort zone to pay her more attention and dance a bit to her tune. She and

Tope would have been a fantastic pair. She is lively, as her dad was. As soon as eyes were opened in the morning, a plan was quickly forming in her brain as to where to go and what to do to get the best enjoyment out of the time. This applied to Tope when he was alive and to my daughter now. The beauty of a lie-in Saturday morning was totally lost on him and also on my daughter. She always wants to get up and go somewhere. If Tope were alive today, they would have had a lot of daddy-and-daughter outings, and I would have enjoyed the peace of being left out of it. As a young lady in my late teens, I had many outings, just my father and I, and they were special moments. I really feel it was an experience every girl should have, especially before they start dating, but sadly it is an experience my daughter will never have.

Chapter 15

Standing Strong and All Alone

In 2013, I had a bit of a health-scare. One evening, as I lay in bed watching tele after a busy day at work, snacking on some peanuts which had become a favourite pastime, one of the nuts seemed to have fallen into my shirt. When I tried to brush it away, I realised that what I thought was a peanut in my shirt was actually a small lump in my left breast. Instinctively, I panicked. I consulted Dr Google, and, from what I gleaned from my research, I was fairly certain that it was nothing to worry about and decided not to fret about it. This was a couple of months before Christmas. Early in the New Year, I decided to visit my GP and report the uninvited visitor in my left breast. I was so sure that the doctor would examine me briefly, tell me it was nothing and send me on my merry way, but he didn't! He looked really worried and sent me to the breast-cancer clinic at our local hospital. I was distraught, but I couldn't tell anybody. Obviously, if Tope had been alive, I would have told him, but, as things were, I had no Tope to tell. I spoke to myself, encouraged myself, convinced myself that the doctor was just being overly cautious. Surely when the specialist staff take a look, they will see that it's nothing: this was the meditation of my heart. After the initial examination in the hospital, I was sent for a mammogram and then for a biopsy. I was still in denial of any bad report and believing that all was well. I had to wait for a week after the biopsy. I still could not tell anyone. I felt it wasn't fair to worry anyone unnecessarily until I was sure there was something to worry about. I had to conceal my fear from my mother, my children and my brother who lived with me at the time. I held my head high, as if I had no problems in this world and just begged God to have mercy on me. By this time in my life, I had become an expert in holding a straight face.

The results of the biopsy came back as inconclusive, so the ordeal of my condition persisted. I was told by the medical staff that I would have to have an operation to extract the lump and get it tested properly. My first thought was, Who will look after me while I'm recuperating from the operation? I am the one that looks after my household, there is no one available to do the same for me. I wanted to say No to the operation, but then one of my friends, Bunor, got involved. I must have told her about one of my appointments. She insisted she would drive me to the hospital for the op and then back home and assist me in any way I needed. She was the angel God had sent to me in that hour. I agreed to the operation, and it was duly scheduled. I still hadn't told anyone in my family, but, on the night before the operation, I told my mother. She insisted it was nothing, but, since I had booked the operation, I should go for it. I got to the hospital nice and early. I was prepped and wheeled into the operating theatre. I was looking around thinking, This is a really scary place, but in a few seconds the anaesthetic had kicked in and I lost consciousness.

By the time I came round, the operation had been done, and I was back on the ward. It felt as if it had just been ten minutes, but in reality it had been about six hours. My friend Bunor came and picked me up and brought me back home. I took three days off work and had to wait two weeks for the results to come back. Those two weeks dragged on and felt like two years, and I missed my Tope even more. Anyway, the results came back after two weeks, and I was given the all clear. It turned out it was nothing, and I wondered why I had to go through that rollercoaster ride.

Chapter 16

Lessons Learned in Paris

It had been a few years since we had been abroad on a family holiday. As I said before, I was never one to want to go away, I was quite content to stay at home with a good book or a good movie. Nonetheless, I am eternally grateful to my friends that dragged me from one holiday destination or the other over the years. These holidays exposed my children to the world, and I thank God for them. On this occasion, I had to plan the holiday all by myself. I needed a holiday in which I didn't have to be responsible for the entertainment. After giving it some thought, I decided Disneyland, Paris, would do the trick. It was close enough not to be too expensive, and we could get there without even getting to the airport. I booked a five-day stay in one of the Disney hotels, and we were due to go out there in the summer of 2014.

The children were sufficiently excited about it, which was good, because it wasn't always easy to find something that they would both want to do. On the morning of the trip, my brother Tomi drove us to St Pancras station, and we boarded the Eurostar to Paris. We were there in a mere three hours. Getting through security was quite tedious, but eventually we made it to our accommodation. I needed a hotel-room with a fridge, just because I loved my cold drinks at every hour of the day. I had paid extra at the point of booking for a room with a fridge, but when we got to the room there was no fridge. Not a good start. The children didn't want me to rock the boat, as they had fallen in love with our room on sight, but there is no way I would have enjoyed my stay if I couldn't have a cold drink at midnight. However, the hotel staff were very good and, as soon as I mentioned the error, they gave us an identical room but one with the needed fridge! We were all happy and finally satisfied. I had booked three meals a day and unlimited access to the parks for five days, so we could all go and come as we pleased, meeting up at meal times.

I wasn't much for the parks, but, as I was here in Euro Disney, I thought I might as well check it out and see how much of it I remembered from my honeymoon.

First of all, I went out with my daughter, but it quickly became apparent that the rides she liked and wanted to go on were very different from what I could tolerate; and what I was interested in she found very boring. We soon went our separate ways, and I was all on my own.

There were thousands of people in the Disney Park, queuing for rides, eating snacks, shopping, taking pictures, laughing and generally having a good time. I was on my own, and, for the first time in a very long time, I felt lonely! Fancy that, I was in the midst of thousands of people, yet I felt all alone!! The last time I was in this park, I was a new bride and I had the love of my life by my side. I was prepared to go on every single ride he suggested. I was in a big crowd but quite oblivious of them, I had eyes only for my husband, and I was deliriously happy to be there with him.

This experience of loneliness taught me a lesson. For me to be okay and not continually feel a sense of loss or lack, I need to plan ahead and avoid situations where my singleness was thrust in my face. You've got to understand that I did not choose to be single and that it was my plan to grow old and grey with Tope. Since that has not happened and I fail to see a replacement for him anywhere in sight, I really must guard my heart, so that I don't continue to trigger ill-feelings of loneliness or depression. I plan where I go and with whom I go and whether I need to be going at all. If it is a place where there are going to be lots of couples, especially couples that I do not know, then it might be a good idea for me to just stay away and not cause myself any grief. This is not to say I wish these couples any ill-will. It's just that what they have magnifies what I do not have, but rather wished I did have.

Alone in the park, I learnt a lesson. This was more than ten years after Tope had died, and I am still learning lessons about how to live without him. To think that we were only married for a mere six years, and his life certainly impacted on mine in a tremendous way. Apart from the fact that I have two beautiful children that forever ties me to him, he developed a part in me that no one since has come near to touching. I am a different person because of my connection to Tope, both in his life time and beyond his life. God is truly amazing. I really do believe that Tope was my soulmate and I know what I had with him was special and can never be replaced.

On one of the days, while we were out there in Paris, I took the kids into the city to visit the Eiffel Tower and see some of the sights of Paris. This was one of the days that we actually enjoyed each other's company outdoors as a family - an experience that I remember with a smile in my heart. After about five days in Paris, it was time to return home. As we had taken our trip in the middle of the summer holidays, we still had about a week and a half to relax and catch our breath when we got back to the UK before school and work resumed.

Tara Talabi

Chapter 17

Academic Angels

It was almost time for my baby girl to go off to secondary school, and the thought of leaving her at the bus-stop for her to make her way to school on her own filled me with trepidation. I had no problem with her geographical prowess: my concern was that she talked too much and might end up talking to every single person on the bus and not getting to her destination on time. Such tardiness just wouldn't do! With this in mind, I was looking for a school that was close enough to where I worked so that I could make sure she got to school on time every day. If I found a good school nearby, not only could I make sure she was in school on time, but she could even come to me at the end of the day and I should be able to bring her home. I visited some schools in my local area and was considering one particular school, which I was really beginning to think might be the right choice. Then I happened to bump into a friend of mine, the same one that swayed me in the decision of my son's school, actually thinking about it now. Ronke and Gbenga, her husband, must have been my children's academic angels. I say this because they always supported me in the most critical times of my children's schooling. It was Ronke that asked me whether I had checked out a particular school for Aramide. As it was at the time, I hadn't looked at the school at all, because I felt it was too far away from where I worked, and I really wanted to keep my daughter close. However, as the said school was quite close to where we lived, I decided to give it a try. I looked up the date for their open evening, and they had only one day left! I had to attend or I should have lost my chance at the school altogether. While at the open day, I promptly decided that this was a good place for my daughter to attend. It was a smallish all-girls Catholic school. There would be no place to hide for Aramide, all her antics would be on full show and could be nipped in the bud before they grew horns. I didn't even consult Aramide as to whether or not she wanted to attend this school. I just filled out all the forms, got them signed and submitted them to their respective places, and then I had to work on Aramide and convince her that it was a good school and a great place for her to attend. She got admission to this school, and, when I was registering her, I had no idea how much of my time I would end up spending at the school in the days and years to come. I must have mentioned it before, Aramide was sent to this world to keep me awake. Looking after Aramide as a child was a full-time wrap-around job. There was certainly no time to snooze or slumber. I got called to Aramide's school so many times that I actually lost count. She was always in some scrape or another: not usually anything serious, but enough to get her in trouble and me called out of work. She was undoubtedly a really boisterous child, feisty, opinionated, loud and often distracted. Her focus was usually on the wrong thing, not on what her teacher was saying. Every teacher she ever had knew she was a handful. Even my dad, God rest his soul, nicknamed her Hurricane because that best described her character as a toddler. Anyway, this story is my memoir, not hers.

Aramide went off to secondary school, while Ayomide went off to college to do a BTec in business studies. Once again, I must commend my academic angels. Gbenga coached Ayomide in mathematics and helped to ensure he got the right grades to get into college. Ayomide was a very laid-back student, and, as soon as he was old enough to organise his own academic affairs, he stopped involving me. This was quite difficult for me because, Ayomide being my first child, I wasn't really experienced in what to do or where to go regarding school offers and admissions. I was mostly finding out things after the fact and not before. For instance, in the season of seeking out the right college for him, we had both considered a few and gone together to visit them. But on the day the GCSE results were published and my boy got his needed credits, he told me he was off to register in college, and it was not one of the ones we had visited; it was a different one. At the end of the day, he came home, having enrolled at a college that he was happy with, quite far away from home; I had never even heard of it. I later on researched it, and it turned out to be a good college, but how and when he chose it I had no idea. He repeated the pattern when choosing a university. All I remember was that he had chosen one university, he had been granted admission, and I had to pay a deposit for his campus accommodation. He did all the ground-work himself and required only my signature as his parent.

Chapter 18

Adieu, Mum

My mother's health was waning, and it was heart-breaking to watch. During all my years growing up as a child, my mother had been very strong: physically, mentally, emotionally and intellectually. There was not a thing that my mother put her mind to that she did not achieve. Even in this dreadful illness, she took a very strong stance and fought for her life. A lesser person would certainly not have made it as far as she did. She refused to give up and die. She fought a good fight. The time she did have was well used. She attended a Bible school online; she attended some school of ministry in person every Sunday after church in Ilford. She got involved with her local Anglican church around the corner from her house. (She had also taken me there one Wednesday when I was on leave from work.) She got involved in some prison outreach and used to go in and preach to the inmates. She even made friends with some of them; some, after they were released, became her pals. These were all the things she had wanted to pursue earlier on in life but circumstances did not allow. I watched her doing all this, regardless of her condition, and I was proud of her strength and resilience. I supported her by picking up her administrative tasks, printing out her handouts and emailing her registration forms and assignments. It was as if she thought that, since she only had a short time, she would do as much as she could. And then it felt rather sudden, but maybe it wasn't really: she fell ill and really had to slow down. In fact, everything kind of ground to a halt. She couldn't eat and so had no energy to move, and that was the beginning of the end really. She became very frail and fragile, and, after a while, even standing up became a challenge. One Saturday evening, she called me and asked me whether I remembered to get her some agave which she used as a sweetener for her tea. I said I would bring it to church for her on Sunday morning. The next day, when she woke up too ill to come to church, I drove down to see her after church, and she had lost consciousness. My darling mother, Mrs Olugbeminiyi Oduntan Olajumoke Afanu, née Mabogunje, died in the early hours of the next day, 1 February 2016. I was devastated. For once, I felt life had something against me. Why, at less than fifty years of age, had I lost my husband, my father and now my mother? Why, Lord: was this my lot? Was I not worthy of being loved, cherished and looked after? I still wanted the companionship of my husband, and I also wanted the covering of my mother's prayers and support. Why had they all left me before I was ready to let go? I felt as if I had to grow up very quickly, whether I liked it or not. I felt as if even my children were cheated out of their grandparents. Thank God they got to know my parents, even if only for a short while. I was married before I lost all my grandparents. I knew all four of them quite well. My children's paternal grandparents were dead before they were born, and both my parents were gone while they were quite young. Yes, I know it, life is not fair. I have tried to make my children understand this, but it never quite rings true until you experience the injustice of this unfair life. For me, my faith has kept me going. My trust and hope in God have kept my head above water all these years. His favour, mercy and unending love were so evident when I lost my husband that I felt guilty complaining. I really did feel engulfed in God's loving arms in my journey of recovery from my loss. Regardless of this, I still yearn for what I have lost. My parents were still happily married and living together when my dad died. Then my mother came to live with us in London, and I delighted in providing for her and giving her all she ever wanted. Even though I had the pleasure of doing it, it lasted for only a few years. I guess I should be grateful that I had that opportunity. My daughter was young and once asked me, 'Mum, why are you always buying things for grandma?' Smiling, I told her that this is how we show love and appreciation for our parents who sacrificed for us when we were young and that I expected her (my daughter) to do the same for me some day.

I had to cry just a little bit, then wipe my eyes and bury my mother in the style expected of a good Nigerian child. My Nigerian culture dictated burying my parent in a certain fashion. It entailed a lot of things. I had to gather my siblings and start planning. We planned, and I think we did a good job. We had the support of Dr Cole, mum's friend, ever present. Our church, Glory House, also stood with us. Friends and family were very supportive as well. They all chipped in financially to make the burden light. This is our culture, it's the way you do things. When you visit someone who is bereft, you always give a monetary gift to help them with funeral bills or just to support living post-bereavement. So we sent my mother off in style, and in many instances I wished I could phone her up and tell her who gave us money or who came all the way from the U.S., from Nigeria, from Manchester and all the other places people arrived from to attend her funeral. It was a grand send-off, and, even though it cost a large amount of money, I have no regrets at all. I think my mother would have said, Well done, my children. About a year after the funeral, I ordered a marble headstone for her grave and had it erected. It had to be done after this length of time so that the ground could set and withstand its weight.

Shortly after this, I took a trip to Nigeria, mainly to go and tidy up my mother's house and affairs. To my surprise, my mother had already put her house in order, so to speak. She had bagged up most of her clothes and given away the big household goods like freezers and fridges, so clearing up was not too difficult. Emotionally it was tough, but what had to be done had to be done. I cleared away as much as I could and took a big bag of clothes to the less fortunate in the village. I used the rest of the time to visit aunties and uncles that I hadn't seen in years and generally had a nice time on my summer trip to Nigeria.

One of my main comforts during this time was the bond I had with my siblings and their spouses. There are six of us: my brother and his wife, Timi and Kemi, my next brother, Tomi, my sister and her husband, Tinuke and Demola, and of course myself. I do not know where I would be without them. We value the relationship we have with one another and delight in coming together to have a good time or addressing issues. We are also there for each other when needed. I can call on anyone of the men at any time and be certain that they will take my concerns seriously and do their best to fix whatever the issue is. The same goes for my sisters. We have shared babysitting, shopping and emotional and spiritual support, and it's just very reassuring that we are available for one another.

I'm really a grown-up now. It's not a joke. I do not have a mother or father; yes, I'm effectively orphaned now. Even though I have my siblings, I do not have a husband, so now I'm actually an orphaned widow: nobody for me to look up to with the assurance that everything is going to be all right. It's just me and God now. This is my life. I must say I have learnt to trust God more now. I have had no choice. He has been my rock, my ever-present help in time of need. His grace has been sufficient for me.

In my new adult stance, I decided I needed a pay rise. I put my mind to finding out how I could do this.

It wasn't going to be easy in my current job, because I had reached the top of my pay-scale; but I knew that if I did some staff development, a course here or there, this might improve my prospects. As it happened, a brilliant course came across my email. It was going to cost me quite a bit of money and almost two years to complete, but, thinking this was the time to invest in my future, I took the bull by the horns, dug into my savings, paid for the course and registered, trying not to look back. I must confess, it was harrowing going back to that level of schooling, especially while working full-time, but I was committed to it now and determined to finish and finish well. My next eighteen months were rigorous study. The course was linked to my job, and so you had to do it on the job. It was really exhausting coming back from work, having a quick meal, then sitting down to study. I would normally be there from around 6.30pm till close to midnight on most weekday nights. By the time I was turning the corner at the end of the course, I had had enough; I really wanted to pack it in. It took all my will-power to complete it, and I'm glad I did: it really paid off when I needed it to.

Tara Talabi

Chapter 19

God's Grace and Mercy

At the end of 2019, I took a Christmas trip to Nigeria. This time I took my children with me. In fact, my siblings and their families came, too, and we made a large family trip of it. The children were now old enough to appreciate the facts about their roots. They were born and bred in the UK, but their cultural heritage and traditions emanated from Nigeria, and I felt they needed to know what their ethnic origin was all about. The first night we stayed in a posh five-star hotel. The children loved it and didn't want to move on to the next location because they were so comfortable. Then we moved to Ijebu-Ode, an old city that seemed to be covered with red sand. We stayed with my aunty, Mrs Oyejide. She lived in a very big house in the middle of not much at all. But once you entered the gates of her compound, you were oblivious to the red dusty roads that you had just left behind. Once again, we were very comfortable, and the children got to see the Christmas turkey alive before it became Christmas dinner. We attended a big annual family meeting on Boxing Day. This was the highlight of the trip. I come from a very large family, and as many of us as possible gather together on Boxing Day, just to be together and thank God for the year past as well as the year to come. The day after that, my siblings and I and all the kids took ourselves off to a local tourist-attraction called Olumo Rocks (they are natural rocks that have formed on top of each other for hundreds of years). We climbed the rock as far as we could go. Some of us in the group actually got to the very top. I didn't, I had had enough half way through. We took lots of photographs and even drank palm wine out of calabashes, the real indigenous way to drink it. We visited the gift-shop and were wowed by the things they had on offer, most of which were too large to consider bringing back to the UK. We did, however, pick up a few small bits as keepsakes to remember our trip by. After having a thoroughly enjoyable day at the Rocks, we found ourselves a local outdoor restaurant and introduced the kids to native foods they hadn't had before. Their initial response was rejection, because it was so unfamiliar, but they actually ended up enjoying it when they gave it a go. We ate so much, their portions being much larger in Nigeria than what we were used to in the UK; but, after having our fill and a totally fulfilling day, we dispersed to our different locations for the night.

Our next Nigerian adventure happened within the next few days. We took a trip to a remote beach in Lekki. When I say 'remote', it felt as if it must have been on the very tip of the shores of Lagos. We travelled through civilised communities and kept going till we left all civilisation behind and still weren't there yet. When we eventually got there, it seemed as if we had reached the end of Lagos and were about to drive into the Atlantic Ocean! We went in a large group of about fifty-five people, and we were the only ones on this large beach of fine white sand: no other human beings but us! I felt a bit as if I were one of the crew of the Swiss Family Robinson, except that we were not lost and had all our vehicles parked up and ready to take us back to civilisation. We had taken with us lots of food and snacks like Jollof rice, fried chicken, cakes, crisps, popcorn and cold soft drinks and some not-so-soft drinks. We also took board-games, beach-balls and everything to keep us entertained while we were there. Needless to say, we had a big picnic on the beach and, having eaten our fill, we ventured near the sea and dipped our toes in. Sometimes the water came in so fast it progressed way above our feet to our waists. It was lots of fun and an experience my children will never forget. We had one more family party that we attended in Lagos on New Year's Day, and then we returned to the UK on 2nd January. It was a really successful trip, and I thank God for the time spent out there with friends and family. I am so glad I took my children to Nigeria at that particular time, because this was just before the dreaded pandemic that shook the world.

We all returned to school and work in January, and life seemed to be progressing as normal until the pandemic hit and everything went a bit crazy. Schools closed, then opened up again to the vulnerable and first responders' children; churches went online; shops limited the number of customers indoors and caused long queues on the outside to get in; flour became a scarce commodity in London because we were all at home baking cakes and everybody put on a few pounds. Large gatherings were prohibited, and there were all sorts of sanctions in place in a bid to keep everyone safe.

At the beginning of the Covid season, I was working from home, and it was truly horrendous. I felt as if work had invaded my private space. I had never been one to take work home before, but now it seemed work had followed me home whether I allowed it or not. Thankfully, it only lasted for a week or two before I got called back to work. Lock-down to me from then on meant slightly modified working-hours not working from home. Working in a school meant there was always some child that needed the school's support, and such support needed to be administered from school, not from my home. This meant I was quite busy during the so-called lock-downs and never really isolated. I made sure I had my Covid jabs as soon as I was called, because I was always out of my house: if I wasn't at work, I was in Sainsbury's or even at church. I was never really locked down. By the end of May, the lockdown had been lifted, but there where so many restrictions that we might as well have been still locked down. Social distancing, rule of six, hospitality lock-down, Zoom meetings, hand-sanitizer, gloves and face-masks became the order of the day. It seemed as if overnight life had changed drastically. You could no longer just hug a friend in the street, and, if anyone coughed near you, it caused panic. The slightest head-ache you had you feared the worst, and self-test Covid kits became really popular. Through it all, I was saved from the horrible infection, but it seemed to be everywhere, and the news was horrendous, so many people were dying. Only the supermarkets seemed to be opened; everything else was in lock-down. There was no church, except online; no cinemas; restaurants (at one point), libraries, theatres and gyms were all shut down. It made socialising quite difficult, and Zoom became the champion. I got quite used to it and kind of enjoyed the fact that I didn't have to go anywhere over the weekend.

Chapter 20

Turning Fifty

Summer was fast approaching, and school was closing down as well for a well-needed break. My birthday was round the corner, but Covid had ensured that I couldn't have a lavish party under the circumstances. I secretly revelled in this fact, because I really I didn't want something big at all; but it was my fiftieth birthday, and all my family and friends expected me to celebrate it in style. As I was on holiday from work, I had a lot of time to think about it. Some restrictions had been lifted, and we were allowed to have a gathering up to thirty people in a garden; so this was exactly what I did. I had planned and scheduled a Zoom party for my birthday, and my sister promised to send me a photographer in the morning of the day; she insisted I was ready before the photographer arrived. I was ready. The door bell went, and my daughter said I should open the door. I found this as bit strange but I obliged. I opened the door, and there stood a guy with a trumpet and a music-box, playing 'Happy Birthday' to me. There was a lady behind him with a very large gift hamper in her hands and a wide grin from ear to ear. There was someone else with a large birthday-cake as well, all of them wishing me 'Happy Birthday'. It wasn't a photographer at all!

I invited them in and immediately started to dance to the jazz music playing for me, still unsure whether I knew these ladies or not. They seemed to know me. They came bearing gifts, cake and music, so I danced. At one point they stopped the music and asked me to open my card. When I did, I realised that they were sent to me by my siblings, who had organized the whole thing with my children. I was so touched that I wasn't sure whether to laugh or cry. It was such a pleasant surprise.

After they left, I got ready for the Zoom party. I had over a hundred attendees, and it lasted for about an hour. It was actually quite lovely, I didn't even think I had a hundred friends who would agree to link up, but

I certainly did! Because it was a Zoom party, it allowed family and friends from far and near to attend that wouldn't have been able to attend otherwise. After the Zoom party, the children and I went out to dinner, which was paid by for my brother. On the weekend I had a garden party in my little garden, and only my immediate family and a few close friends were present to make sure we didn't go over the thirty-people quota. I had some gazebos set out in the garden. I rented some party chairs, erected some birthday banners, set up a food table in one corner, a big drum of cold drinks in the other corner, and not even the rain could hold back my joy and excitement on the day. My sister had organised a professional make-up artist to come and make me look pretty, and she did a stunning job: I really looked the part of a radiant celebrant. We took lots of pictures and even videos to remember the event. It was a small and intimate gathering and turned out to be a really lovely party, one of the best I have ever had.

So now I've turned fifty, this is my story. I am joyful now. I think I have recovered from the shadows caused by the dark clouds of life. It's been a journey, it's left its scars, but truly joy comes in the morning when you put your trust in God. When I tell you my life is like an open book, you can believe me: it is all here in black and white for you to see. I have laid all bare to encourage someone; to inform someone that life has its twists and turns and doesn't have to end just because you meet a very sharp bend in the road. When Tope died, I wanted to die also, but for my children I knew I had to live, I knew I had to move on and smile again. My children deserved a complete and well-rounded mother. I believe one of the reasons God blessed me with the children was to make sure I carried on.

Every human being on earth has multiple purposes for their existence whether they were planned to be on earth or not. I believe once God has allowed us entry, he assigns purpose to us and, as the purpose is being fulfilled, there will be a resultant peace that follows. Now that I'm in my fifties, I'm taking a closer look at my life and searching for destiny assignments. I have discovered that I actually have a voice and can reach out to widows and solo mums, to encourage and instruct on the art of living and smiling again after bereavement or loss. In this virtual age I can communicate with anyone in any part of the world without leaving my house. I have started reaching out to anyone I'm led to. A letter, a text message, a hug or even a smile is sometimes all that someone needs to feel better, and I am committed to doing my little bit to help someone through a difficult patch.

I have also discovered the menopause, and it's nothing like what I thought it was. Trust me, it can be much more than hot flushes, but that's a whole new book for another day and you'll just have to wait for me to get that book published so I can tell you all about that journey.

Tara Talabi

About Tara Talabi

Tara Talabi is who I am. A Christian, British Nigerian woman, mother of 2 young adults, married at 27 and widowed by the age of 33. My story tells you of my life's journey from a joy filled childhood through to the darkness of widowhood and then to peace, acceptance and progress into middle age.

I have essentially for the most part, spent my life looking out for my children, making sure they had all they needed regardless of the fact that they didn't have a dad. They are grown up now and do not need me as much, and I feel now, it is time for me to spread my wings and soar. I love to watch movies, read, write and cook exotic dishes while socializing with family and friends.

In my head and in my heart, I am first and foremost a Christian and this tends to influence my likes and dislikes for instance the movies I watch and the books I read. I cringe at excessive swearing, killing, sexual content, racism, paranormal/horror and general wickedness. I love most forms of Christian fiction, period drama as well as modern day, romance, family mysteries and biographies of interesting people.

I have worked full time as an administrator in primary education for over 20 years.

Connect with Tara Talabi

www.pneumasprings.co.uk/product/joy-comes-in-the-morning/

Reviews

If you are looking for story of hope, encouragement and assurance, this is a good book to read. You will cry, laugh and truly see God's grace in Tara's life. It's a compilation of some of the events that have taken place in the life of a very courageous woman and how her trust in God with her beautiful support-system brought her to a place where she can confidently say, Joy truly comes in the morning!

Pastor Abosede Odulele

It is a book that touches the key nerves of life and how, through simplicity of mind and action, God has helped Tara navigate the complexities of life without losing her joy.

Dipo Akinrinlade – Author of *Everyone Can: Taking personal responsibility for your financial future.*

Mourning turns to joy at dawn -
Publishedbestseller.com